Cover photo; the grave markers of George Giles
Vincent and Emilia Elizabeth Vincent in the north
cloister of Westminster Abbey.

Photo by Kim Tame

Contents

Table of figures

Preface

In the summer of 2008, I arrived at Helena House, Brownlow Road, Reading, Berkshire (UK), to start a new job, for Prospects, a Christian organisation specialising in the support of adults with learning disabilities.

I joined a lovely team of caring and committed Christians, who did their best, despite very tight funding, to support the people in their care with compassion and humanity. Two years later, I was the manager. Part of my role was to manage the house itself; repairs and maintenance soon proved to be an ongoing challenge. This Victorian house, or rather, three interconnected houses, was beautiful in parts, especially the part known as North House. Helena House had been extended and adapted for later standards, not always well. The water tanks gurgled and the massive boilers were expensively reaching the ends of their lives. Plumbers muttered phrases like "never seen anything like it" as they inspected the tortuous route the pipes took from the bathroom to the drains. When some ceilings had to be replaced, the work exposed lathe and plaster and the insulation from a previous generation – bales of hay. But the house, shabby in places as it was, was a happy place for the people who lived there.

I started looking into the history of Helena House when one of the staff came to me with concerns that some of the night staff were afraid of certain parts of the building; they thought it was haunted. I had done sleep-in shifts there myself and had never seen anything more frightening than myself in the mirror. But one lady had a fear of the cupboard under the stairs, and another was convinced that she had heard a strange voice one night. Another colleague thought that a previous resident, who had died in hospital, still occupied his old room. When it was proposed to make that room the staff sleep-in room, several colleagues refused to sleep in there.

A Google search in an idle moment came up with the records of the 1901 census and the 24 women who lived there. 24 women? I'll confess, my first thought was "brothel." But I read on. A Miss Frances Ransome was listed as head of household; then there were four nurses, five servants and 13 patients.

As I investigated further, I found out that Helena House had been in the business of caring for people for over a century. I knew snippets already; that prior to being taken over by Prospects, the house had been a home for widows of Anglican clergymen. One room had been used as a chapel; there is still, at the time of writing, a cross on the roof at the rear of the building. And when, months later, I had the time to do a bit more research, there was more; Helena House had been a place of specifically Christian care, with close links with nearby All Saints' Church, almost since the house was built. Many people had died there, but they had died surrounded by loving, Christian care.

Further research would lead me to the forgotten founder of the Helena Nursing Home; Miss Emilia Vincent.

Following the trail of census records, birth, marriage and death records and newspaper reports, I have pieced together an account of Emilia's life, from her birth in the community of Westminster Abbey, to her death in Reading, Berkshire. The lives she interacted with include royalty, aristocracy and country gentry, to the tradespeople and local politicians of Reading; I also discovered the poignant story of a little original Canadian girl who lived for just a short time in Emilia's care.

This is a historical study of a real person, and of real places; a London that has all but disappeared, and a

Reading that is, in parts, still recognisable. Culture, customs and language have evolved since the 19th century. In places, I have quoted sources that used the terminology of the time; some of this terminology is now recognised as inappropriate and/or offensive. Where I quote the original sources, the intention is to be factual, not to give offence. In places, I have used poetic licence to fill in the details of lives and events. I do this to present a realistic and interesting depiction of events, not to mislead.

Finally, a note about notes! For ease of reading, I have used end notes solely to provide references; all relevant information is in the body of the text. You can safely ignore the endnotes unless you want to follow up the sources.

Kim Tame

April 2022

Part One; Westminster

Chapter one: Emilia Vincent - child of the Abbey

The year is 1828; the month is October. The King is George IV; but not for much longer. The King is obese, almost blind from cataracts, and in constant pain from gout and bladder issues, unable to lie down, and kept going by means of alcohol and laudanum. He has slightly less than another two years of life to struggle through.

Arthur Wellesley, 1st Duke of Wellington, the military hero who led the allied forces to defeat Napoleon Bonaparte, is the Prime Minister. The Dean of Westminster is Dr. John Ireland.

In Regent's Park, a brand-new zoological garden has just opened as a centre for scientific research, though it is not yet open to the public. There is a brand-new hospital in London, the London General Institution for the Gratuitous Care of Malignant Diseases – later to become the Royal Free Hospital. London also has a brand-new college, King's College. Meanwhile in Edinburgh, a shadier side of the medical world is about to be exhumed, with the trial of the notorious grave-robbers, William Burke and William Hare. Mary Anning is collecting fossils along the Dorset coast, and Sir Walter Scott is the most popular modern novelist. Twenty-year-old Charles Dickens is working as a legal clerk, and has yet to begin his writing career.

In the heart of the city of Westminster, a family gathers at the font of St. John's Church, Smith Square. Mr. and Mrs George Giles Vincent have brought their three-week-old baby girl to be baptised by her uncle, Rev. William St. Andrew Vincent, the vicar at All Hallows in Thames Street. He takes the baby from her nursemaid and baptises her in the name of the Father, Son and Holy Ghost, according to the Book of Common Prayer.

Her name is Emilia, after her mother. Nearby, Emilia's grandparents, James and Margaret Tappenden, look proudly on at their large family; five sons may have disappointed them in not producing grandchildren, but four of their five daughters have large families of their own. Three of their adult children live with them in Millbank Street; Sophia Frances, James' daughter from his first marriage, who is now widowed, and Jenkin Edward and Jemima Rachel Tappenden, who remain unmarried.

Their sister, Emilia Elizabeth, married well; George Giles Vincent is a solicitor and Westminster Abbey's Chapter Clerk and registrar, the most senior lay employee. There are two children from his first marriage; Hannah is now 24, and as the eldest daughter, a vital support to her stepmother and four half-siblings.

George junior is 21. George has followed his father into the law and is also an administrator of Westminster Abbey. He has the role of Steward of the Manors of Westminster; managing the abbey's far-flung farming estates, and the income generated from them.

Hannah may have some hazy memories of her own mother, Mary Worsley; and George probably none at all, since she died when he was only three months old.

Emilia Elizabeth's older children gather round the new baby; Francis (10), Thomas (9) and Mary (6).

If Uncle William St. Andrew Vincent is performing the baptism, then no doubt his wife, Aunt Fanny, is there too, along with their adult daughters, Josepha Mary and Frances Ann, who are not yet married. Their sons are busy studying; William junior is at Christ Church College, Oxford, studying to become a priest and John Francis attends the East India Company Military

Seminary at Addiscombe, Surrey, training for military service in India.

Emilia is blessed to be born into a large and supportive family; in her early years, she has five older siblings and half-siblings, grandparents, aunts, uncles and cousins for company and friendship, in addition to the community of Westminster Abbey and the motley assortment of schoolboys, clergy, aristocracy and lawyers who live around Dean's Yard and the Cloisters.

Not far from the shelter of the Abbey community is all the excitement and danger of a rapidly changing and expanding London.

Emilia will outlive a remarkable century; she'll go from homes lit with candles and oil lamps to gaslights and on to electricity. She'll see horse-drawn vehicles give way to steam and internal combustion, chamber pots and privies to flushing water closets connected to mains sewers. She'll live through the entire reigns of William IV, Queen Victoria and King Edward VII.

She'll follow the exponential growth of medical discoveries with increasing delight; nursing becomes established as a respectable profession for women, doctors start to abandon miasma theory – the long-held belief that disease is carried by bad smells or fog –and discover some of the real causes of disease. The arrival of germ theory will pave the way for some real and effective interventions and treatments. Women will even start to become doctors. The rising use of chloroform makes childbirth a less risky proposition, and the dawn of the importance of good hygiene even more so.

But Emilia is a baby. All this is still to come.

Chapter two; The changing city of Westminster

"There are multitudes who believe that Westminster is a city of palaces, of magnificent squares, and regal terraces; that it is the chosen seat of opulence, grandeur and refinement; and that filth, squalor, and misery are the denizens of other and less favoured sections of the metropolis. The error is not in associating with Westminster much of the grandeur and splendour of the capital, but in entirely dissociating it in idea from the darker phases of metropolitan life. As the brightest lights cast the deepest shadows, so are the splendours and luxuries of the west-end found in juxtaposition with the most deplorable manifestations of human wretchedness and depravity. There is no part of the metropolis which presents a more chequered aspect, both physical and moral, than Westminster. The most lordly streets are frequently but a mask for the squalid districts which lie behind them, whilst spots consecrated to the most hallowed of purposes are begirt by scenes of indescribable infamy and pollution; the blackest tide of moral turpitude that flows in the capital rolls its filthy wavelets up to the very walls of Westminster Abbey; and the law-makers for one-seventh of the human race sit, night after night, in deliberation, in the immediate vicinity of the most notorious haunt of law-breakers in the empire. There is no district in London more filthy and disgusting, more steeped in villainy and guilt, than that on which every morning's sun casts the sombre shadows of the Abbey, mingled, as they soon will be, with those of the gorgeous towers of the new "Palace at Westminster.""

The "Devil's Acre," as it is familiarly known in the neighbourhood, is the square block comprised between Dean, Peter, and Tothill Streets, and Strutton Ground. It is permeated by Orchard Street, St. Anne's Street, Old and New Pye Streets, Pear Street, Perkins' Rents, and

Duck Lane. Some of these narrow, covered passageways lead into small quadrangular courts, containing but a few crazy, tumble-down-looking houses, and inhabited by characters of the most equivocal description. The district, which is small in area, is one of the most populous in London, almost every house being crowded with numerous families, and multitudes of lodgers. There are other parts of the town as filthy, dingy, and forbidding in appearance as this, but these are generally the haunts more of poverty than crime. But there are none in which guilt of all kinds and degrees converges in such volume as on this, the moral plague-spot not only of the metropolis, but also of the kingdom. And yet from almost every point of it you can observe the towers of the Abbey peering down upon you, as if they were curious to observe that to which they seem to be indifferent[1]."

Emilia may or may not have read that description of the Devil's Acre, written by Alexander MacKay for Charles Dickens' publication *"Household Words"*; but even if not, she would have recognised the truth in his description. She grew up to be familiar with the staggering contrasts of Westminster; the very rich and very poor often side by side.

Emilia would often have gone to visit her mother's parents, James and Margaret Tappenden at 59 Millbank Street. In the company of her parents, governess or older siblings — for part of their route would have been far too disreputable for children to walk unaccompanied — she would have walked through a Westminster very different from today's; the iconic outline of the Houses of Parliament was not there. There was no Clock Tower housing the great bell, Big Ben, no Methodist Central Hall, no Broad Sanctuary. No Treasury building. No Westminster Cathedral.

Figure 1; Westminster Abbey from Dean's Yard, by Herbert Railton[2]

Leaving their home close to Westminster Abbey, the Vincents would have walked through Dean's Yard, the boundaries of which were marked by rows of houses that would not be recognised by modern visitors. Dean's Yard was yet to be substantially rebuilt on three sides; Church House would replace the terraces on the south side, George Gilbert Scott's terrace of eight houses would appear to the north and Westminster Choir School and new boarding houses for Westminster School on the west side.

They may have taken a short-cut that no longer exists; Flood Street was a small road connecting Dean's Yard with Tothill Street, its name bearing witness to the risks taken when the Thames overflowed. Flood Street was not large — the house numbers went no higher than six — but there were at least two substantial establishments.

One was the Coach and Horses inn at number four. There was once a rumour that the famous Lady Emma Hamilton, mistress of Lord Nelson, had been a barmaid there, but was dismissed for misconduct[3]. But in the 1830s and 40s, Mr. Davidson and Mr. Quye ran a large and respectable establishment where many of the coroner's inquests for the city of Westminster were held; many of them chaired by the Emilia's future brother-in-law, Charles St. Clare Bedford Esq., who was the coroner for Westminster 1845-1888.

The other substantial establishment in Flood Street was the livery stable at number three. This was a compact yard, enclosed with folding gates, containing stabling for 15 horses, standing for three carriages, a grain store, haylofts, chaffroom, and a pump of spring water nearby. The adjacent house comprised six rooms, kitchen and cellars[4].

By 1848, Flood Street was due to disappear completely; it was to be demolished to make way for the new Victoria Street. The last licensee of the Coach and Horses, Mr. Scott, transferred the licence to a new establishment round the corner in Dean Street. The livery yard ceased to trade and the stables were let for a time as cheap lodgings.

On the way along Flood Street, the Vincents might have noted an Irish family who moved into the old stables; Michael and Mary Rohan and their four children. It could hardly have escaped their notice that so many of the city's population lived in a way very different from their own; their poverty as obvious as the rags they wore. The Rohans had escaped the extreme poverty of rural Ireland – at the time when Ireland's rural poor lived barely a step up from mud huts — only to substitute it for the extreme poverty of Westminster, their stable dwelling a small step up from living on the streets. Michael Rohan was visually-impaired and partially paralysed, and unfit to work, so Mary provided for the family by cleaning the offices of the Queen Anne's Bounty charity in Dean's Yard. They did receive some support from their well-to-do neighbours; the Rev. Mr. Repton visited them, and when the family fell ill in 1848, he sent for a doctor to see them[5].

An alternative route out of Dean's Yard, other than along Flood Street, was through the arched gate into Broad Sanctuary, past the gloomy churchyard adjacent to St. Margaret's Church; this was fenced around with iron railings, with overhanging trees and shrubbery and uneven and falling gravestones. It was used as a playground, short-cut and frequently a urinal by the boys of Westminster School and the general public.

Instead of the open spaces to be seen today around the abbey, there were houses built right up to the walls next to Poet's Corner, and a row of mews houses close by the other side, at College Mews, another street that disappeared. In its place is College Green, an open space frequently used for the filming of political commentary and news. But the TV reporters of today would not recognise the Palace of Westminster that stood, or rather, didn't, in the 1840s, for it was then a major building site. In 1834, a catastrophic fire, started by careless burning of small wooden tally sticks used for accounting, had almost totally destroyed the old palace. George Gilbert Scott's replacement took more than 30 years to build, with the famous Clock Tower housing Big Ben (the name of the bell) finally completed in 1870.

A few buildings in Parliament Street remained from the 18th century; among them The Red Lion pub, which would have been familiar to Charles Dickens, as well as a great number of that era's prime ministers and politicians. A new Westminster Bridge was planned, and that was completed in 1862.

At Smith Square, we reach the church of St. John the Evangelist. For the Tappendens in Millbank Street, this was their parish church, and it was the church of Emilia Vincent's baptism. It is also the church that Charles Dickens, in *"Our Mutual Friend"*, described as appearing to be "some petrified monster, frightful and gigantic, on its back with its legs in the air."[6] St. John's was also sometimes described as "Queen Anne's footstool;" the story goes that the architect, Thomas Archer, asked the monarch what she wanted the new church to be like. Her Majesty kicked her footstool over and replied, "like that." The less exciting story is that the four towers were added to improve the building's stability in the marshy soil.

Though at the time of building, St. John's was on the edge of the city — west of Lambeth Bridge was open fields — the church served a population that was rapidly expanding. In the early 1800s, it was beautiful and newly refurbished.

The area around St. John's was described by Charles Dickens in *"Our Mutual Friend"*; the house of the dolls' dressmaker is around here somewhere, and the route to Mr. Riah's house in St. Mary Axe can still be walked. It is hard to imagine now that there was once a blacksmith's forge, a timber yard and a dealer in old iron in this area[7]; and Dickens would not recognise St. Mary Axe as it is now, with its high-rise offices and especially the green-glass construction known as the Gherkin.

St. John's churchyard, like other London burial sites, was becoming overcrowded and dangerous. There were so many burials, and so little space for them, that the ground level had risen above the level of the surrounding pavements, and there were fears for public safety. Seven new, large cemeteries opened in the early 19th century; at Kensal Green, West Norwood, Highgate, Abney Park, Brompton, Nunhead and Tower Hamlets.

As the young Vincents reach Millbank Street, they pass through a street of tall houses, some residential and some with shops or workshops on the ground floor. For this was once a street where ordinary people could live, work and learn. Perhaps they stopped to buy their grandparents, Uncle Jenkin, Aunt Jemima and Aunt Sophia some fruit. In the 1840s, you could buy food from the butchers, the grocers, green-grocers, fruiterers, and bakers. You could be fitted for a suit, go to the doctor and buy a hat, and gentlemen could buy cigars and share them with their friends at one of several public houses. In 1842, Robson's London Directory listed, among other businesses;

William West, tobacconist
Edward Cashe, grocer
Blanchard and Son, printers,
William Blackburn, tailor
David Shuter, solicitor
Job Cook, hatter
D. Keogh, Surgeon
Thomas Wyse, greengrocer

Among the pubs were The White Hart, the Robin Hood, the Brewers' Arms, the Brown Bear and the Jolly Miller.

Mr. A. Mallock, tarpaulin manufacturer, was one of those whose business in Millbank Street had done well; well enough for him to educate his son, David, to Master of Arts level. Mr. David Mallock was now in charge of his own school for boys in Millbank Street, and his sisters, Ann and Elizabeth, were running a ladies' academy.[8]

Behind the houses in Millbank Street, the River Thames frontage of the early 19th century was packed with jetties, barges and boats, hauling passengers and cargos of all kinds. From the numerous wharfs – St. Peter's Wharf, Norway Wharf, Dorset Wharf, St. John's Wharf and Union Wharf – cargoes of coal, stone, flour, lime and timber were daily unloaded and delivered across the busy city. Watermen and traders toasted their deals over tankards of ale, crowding onto the wooden verandas of the many pubs that overhung the river, propped up on stilts above the high-water mark. There was, as yet, no Embankment to protect buildings from the highest tides of the Thames. At low tide, the mudlarks scoured the mud and marshy banks, searching the filth and rubbish for anything worth selling.

In the midst of this busy street of merchants and artisans, next door to the school run by the Mallocks, at 59 Millbank Street, lived the elderly couple, James and Margaret Tappenden, with three of their adult children, Sophia Frances Tappenden, the widow of her cousin Francis, Jenkin Edward Tappenden and Jemima Tappenden. Sophia was the daughter of James' first marriage, Jenkin and Jemima were two of James and Margaret's seven children.

Earlier in life, James Tappenden had been rich and influential; but thanks to various failed business ventures, the couple approached the ends of their lives in much reduced circumstances, and no doubt dependent on the Vincents and their extended family for support.

If you walked on to the end of Millbank Street as far as Vauxhall Bridge, you would walk past, not the Tate Britain gallery, but the gloomy hulk of Millbank Prison.

Charles Dickens, in *"David Copperfield,"* describes an "oppressive, sad and solitary" neighbourhood;

"There were neither wharves nor houses on the melancholy waste of road near the great blank prison. A sluggish ditch deposited its mud at the prison walls. Coarse grass and rank weeds straggled over all the

marshy land in the vicinity. In one part, carcases of houses, inauspiciously begun and never finished, rotted away. In another, the ground was cumbered with rusty iron monsters of steam-boilers, wheels, cranks, pipes, furnaces, paddles, anchors, diving-bells, windmill sails... The clash and glare of sundry fiery works upon the river-side arose by night to disturb everything except the heavy and unbroken smoke that poured out of their chimneys. Slimy gaps and causeways... led down through the ooze and slush to the ebb-tide[9]."

Built in 1816, Millbank had been planned by Jeremy Bentham as Britain's National Penitentiary, but it had been plagued by problems from the beginning. Built on marshy soil, the building was subject to subsidence, and for prisoners, the poor diet and susceptibility to a range of infectious diseases led to a most unhealthy environment and a high rate of death. It was decided that Millbank was not suitable for long-term prisoners, and a new National Penitentiary was built at Pentonville. By the 1840s, Millbank was used to house those sentenced to transportation, who typically stayed less than three months. From this convenient position next to the river Thames, hundreds of convicts periodically poured out of its gates and onto the dock to board ships bound for the colonies.

Chapter three; Vincents, Tappendens and Extended Family

Emilia's maternal grandparents, James and Margaret Tappenden were first cousins, and were both related to Rev. William Vincent, D.D., Emilia's paternal grandfather, and the late Dean of Westminster. Margaret's maternal grandmother was Anne Holloway, Dean Vincent's aunt.

The marriage of first cousins was more common then than it is now. James' daughter from his first marriage, Sophia Frances, also married a first cousin, Francis. It was common for families with any kind of property to encourage their offspring to look for marriage among their extended family, in order to ensure inheritances were not watered down by repeated division.

The Tappendens and Vincents were well-matched; upper middle-class, respectable families, who had gained their wealth and position through hard work and successful trade.

Grandfather Vincent

The Rev. Doctor William Vincent, D.D. (1739-1815), came from a family of merchants and clergymen, with family branches in Leicestershire and Ireland. William's father, Giles had been a merchant in goods from Portugal, and for many years, this successful venture provided well for the family. The second son of the family, Giles junior, looked after the Portugal side of the business and lived in St. Martinho, north of Lisbon.

Then a series of disasters ruined the company; first, a principal partner in Lisbon went out of business. Then, towards the end of October 1755, Giles junior decided to travel to Lisbon to send some money home to England. It was the worst possible timing, because the next day, a major earthquake, followed by a tsunami, followed by major fires, struck the Algarve, killing between 30,000 and 50,000 people in Lisbon alone, including Giles Vincent. Then, as if that weren't bad enough, a ship belonging to the company was stolen by its crew.

Francis Vincent, William's eldest brother, carried on the business, but it was never the same again. In William's own words, *"my eldest brother stood his ground as a packer and was the stay of the family. That trade, however, which was one of the best in London, declined so fast, that though he enjoyed the connexions of three or four houses all centred in him, he died a few years ago, respected and in credit, but never enriched by it.[10]"*

William was always grateful for his brother's support; thanks to Francis, he was able to complete his time at Cambridge University, graduate and become an ordained priest of the Church of England. William then spent most of the rest of his life in Westminster. Having been educated at Westminster School from 1748, he returned from Cambridge in 1762 to become an usher (master). He was ordained a deacon in the same year and became a priest in 1765.

William Vincent became under-master at Westminster School, then headmaster in 1788. During this time his most notorious act was having a ploughman mark off 10 acres of Tothill Fields for the use of Westminster School. The area became known as Vincent Square, and this green space is still the playing fields of the school.

It was said that Mr. Vincent had two faults; he lacked humour and he gave an excessive value to routine[11].

Perhaps it was just that he kept his sense of humour well-controlled; John Sergeaunt, in his work, *Annals of Westminster School,* recounted an incident when Mr. Vincent was approached in Dean's Yard by a frail old woman, who begged him for alms. Mr. Vincent gave her half-a-crown and was outraged when a few minutes later, he saw the same old woman with her head being held under the Dean's Yard water pump by two of the boys; Edward Harley, afterwards 5th Earl of Oxford, and William Carey, a future headmaster. Mr. Vincent went to the woman's rescue, and her bonnet fell off, revealing another Westminster pupil – James Hook, afterwards Bishop of Worcester. According to Sergeaunt,

"Vincent was glad to hide his merriment by a precipitate retreat[12]."

His son, George Giles Vincent, shows us a little of his more personal qualities; he described him as "one of the best of parents and best of men," a man who "despised both the parade and the affectation of piety[13]." The Dean believed that Christians should live as though they were prepared at any time to meet death, and doubted the value of death-bed repentance. At the same time, he said that *"none, however, could administer to the afflicted in mind, or on the bed of death, more soothing consolation, or who struggled more against his own emotions at those distressing periods, and more cheerfully, yet devoutly, performed so kind but painful service[14]."*

Mr. Vincent retired from teaching when he was appointed a prebendary of Westminster in 1801, aged 63. In that same year, one of his publications, *"A Defence of Public Education,"* unexpectedly earned him some money, which he good-humouredly handed straight to Hannah, his wife[15]. In 1803, he became Dean of Westminster and in 1807, he also became Rector of Islip, Oxfordshire, and the two posts became linked, thus giving the Dean of Westminster a pleasant country residence – once he had spent around £2,000 on the dilapidated rectory in order to make it so.

The Dean generally spent six months of the year in Islip, where he often preached and actively supported the community, and where he became known for his generosity to the poor. According to his *Gentlemen's Magazine* obituary, he spent his last days *"surrounded by an affectionate family of children and grandchildren, as many blessings of this life as can fall to the lot of a human being[16]."*

Emilia never knew her paternal grandfather, who died before she was born. In hearing the stories of his life, she inherited the sense of gratitude to his brother, her great-uncle Francis. She also inherited a portrait of Francis, which hung in her various homes for the rest of her life. This portrait is now in the possession of the Proprietary House Museum, Perth Amboy, New Jersey, having been donated by the descendants of Emilia's brother, Rev. Thomas Vincent[17].

Grandfather Tappenden

James Tappenden Esq. (1742-1841), might represent the more colourful side of the family. He was a proud man, a chancer, and a social climber; like Dean Vincent, he came from a family of hoymen – merchants.

He worked hard and was successful, as a solicitor, an entrepreneur, a politician and a banker. The substantial funds that came with his marriage to his first wife, Mary Beckwith, must have helped his ambitions, and he was proud to have sent the sons of both his marriages to Rugby School[18]. Mr. Tappenden was a self-made man and rubbed shoulders with the great and the good; but would not always be described as a gentleman himself. One lampoonist described him as *"selfish, scheming and vengeful, and whose arrogance was complemented by the haughtiness of his daughter[19]."* This haughty daughter would be Sophia Frances, his eldest daughter with Mary Beckwith. This Miss Tappenden became Mrs Tappenden when she married her cousin Francis in 1796.

As Mr. Tappenden's fortune grew, so did his reputation, until he gained a prestigious level of trust and respectability. His influence in his hometown, Faversham, Kent, knew no bounds; it was said that he had a finger in every pie in Faversham. As town clerk for many years, he was at the heart of local government. He was at the heart of the business community too, especially once he had opened the Faversham Bank with William Bennett, in 1789. The bank was known as Bennett and Co. for its first ten years but operated from the Tappendens' house, and after Mr. Bennett died, the bank became Tappenden and Co[20]. James Tappenden was joined in the partnership by Francis Tappenden, who was simultaneously his cousin, his brother-in-law, and his son-in-law – thanks to successive intermarriage in the family.

Mr. Tappenden no doubt made the most of the reflected respectability of his extended family. In 1807, Dean Vincent officiated at the wedding, in Faversham, of Anna-Maria, James' first child with his second wife, Margaret, to Major William Samuel Currey of the 54th Regiment of Foot, no doubt introduced to each other by Anna-Maria's brother, Gillow John, who served in the same regiment; they had served together at the Battle of Waterloo[21]. Major Currey later became Lieutenant-Colonel, and on his retirement from the army in 1817, became the Duke of Devonshire's agent in Ireland, at Lismore Castle, near Waterford.[22]

Perhaps Mr. William Newcombe, banker of Fleet Street[23], Dean Vincent's nephew, was also part of their Westminster social circle, and a useful contact in London.

James Tappenden had many business interests and investments, but his downfall was to be his Welsh investment, the Abernant Iron Works, with his nephew/son-in-law, Francis, and subsequently its part in bringing down the Faversham Bank. The Tappendens had poured money into this ambitious venture, funded by loans from their own Faversham Bank. When the iron works failed, so did the bank, and so did James and Francis Tappenden[24].

Figure 2; Faversham Bank banknote, signed by James Tappenden

James and Margaret left Faversham in a hurry, with creditors not far behind, and relocated themselves first to Canterbury, then to Millbank Street, Westminster.

Francis and Sophia went first to Berkshire, where they lived at Mortimer House, near Reading, a property rented by his uncle John, until Francis' death in 1816. His widow Sophia then joined her parents and sister Jemima in Westminster, and died at 59 Millbank Street in 1840.

The reputation of the family suffered; son Charles Octavius Tappenden remained in Faversham and was appointed to most of his father's roles, but was later imprisoned for fraud; Jenkin Edward was imprisoned in London's Fleet Prison, for debt, before he, too went to live at Millbank Street.

Life for their sons might have been precarious at times, but James and Margaret would have been pleased that the future of three of their daughters was secured by highly respectable marriages; Anna-Maria married Major (later Lieutenant-Colonel) Currey, of the 54th Regiment of Foot, and moved to Ireland with him, where they raised five children. Sadly, she died before her parents, at Lismore Castle, near Waterford, in 1827.

Emilia Elizabeth had married the young widower George Giles Vincent, the son of Dean Vincent in 1817.

Then in 1819, their youngest daughter, Louisa Joanna Tappenden, married Rev. Charles Shrubsole Bonnett, at St. John's Church, Smith Square, with Rev. William St. Andrew Vincent officiating. Mr. and Mrs Bonnett lived for the next forty years at his parish at Avington, near Winchester, and raised their family in lush Hampshire countryside.

The evidence suggests this was a close family; the different branches of the family kept in touch, intermarried, supported each other, and assisted each other's careers. The names of the clergymen of the family; William St. Andrew, and later, his son William, and George Giles' son Thomas, and cousins Rev. Stephen Bonnett and Rev. Stephen Terry appear again and again on the certificates for family baptisms, marriages and funerals.

When times were tough, such families supported each other. In those days before a National Health Service, people who needed care were supported by servants or family members at home. After the Poor Law Act of 1834, people who could not work due to age, illness or disability, and had no family to support them, had only the workhouse to turn to, and this was deliberately made the most unpleasant option of all. Only a strong family network prevented such a terrible fate.

Grandmother Margaret Tappenden would live to 86; Grandfather James Tappenden to 99, outliving his daughter Sophia Frances. These three have their final resting places in the over-crowded churchyard of St. John's, Smith Square.

At some point after the deaths of their parents and sister, Jenkin Edward and Jemima Rachel moved around the corner to Great College Street and when they became elderly and frail, in the 1850s, it was another branch of the family, the Terrys at Dummer, that gave them support.

Figure 3; College Street and the wall of the abbey, from a drawing by James Miller, 1781[25]

Emilia's extended family was important to her, and the details available give a glimpse of what middle-to-upper-class life in Victorian England was like; they were educated and eminently respectable, raising sons for the church, the military, medicine and the law; and daughters to be wives of similar. They attended church and had a sense of social responsibility; they supported philanthropy and dutifully served Queen Victoria's empire. In addition to the public records, there are, here and there, some family anecdotes; stories told from one generation to another with drama, humour, and affection.

Vincents of Sussex

Emilia's uncle, William St. Andrew Vincent was the first son of Rev. William Vincent, Dean of Westminster. He attended Westminster School as a King's Scholar, and Christ Church College, Oxford, from 1791. He then became a priest of the Church of England.

In later life, his brother George Giles liked to tell the story of how, in 1803, William travelled to Oakham, Rutland, with a special purpose in mind; he was to marry Frances Elizabeth Gayfere Jones (Fanny). For couples who lived in different parishes, the easiest way to marry was by special licence, rather than wait for the process of the reading of banns in each parish. William duly applied for, and received a special licence, only to discover, on his arrival at Oakham, that he had left it behind in London. He had to write back home and ask for it to be sent by return of post. Two days passed in a state of great anxiety, but the licence was fortunately received just in time for the wedding[26].

William St. Andrew and his brother, George Giles, married the same year, but sadly, George's wife, Mary Worsley, did not survive long after the birth of their third child. In 1817, William officiated at his brother's second marriage, to Emilia Elizabeth Tappenden at St. Margaret's Church, Westminster. He baptized Emilia, his youngest niece, at St. John's Church, Smith Square, in 1828. After serving some years as vicar of All Hallows the Great Church in Thames Street, London, he moved to the quiet countryside of Bolney, Sussex, where he spent many years as Rector. He was also a Canon of Chichester Cathedral.

William and Fanny had four children;

Josepha Mary (1806-1880) married Richard Ignatius Robertson, who was an accountant at the Metropolitan Board of Roads, and private secretary to William Lowther, Second Earl of Lonsdale, who was Postmaster General in Robert Peel's government. The Robertsons lived between two houses, in Devonshire Place, Marylebone, and College Place, Brighton.

Their two sons, Richard Maxwell Gordon Robertson and Vincent Stuart Robertson, both attended Brighton College. Mr. Robertson died from apoplexy (a stroke) at the age of 48 in 1849[27]. Mrs Robertson subsequently sold the London house and all its contents; auctioneers Messrs Rushworth and Jarvis received instructions to sell rosewood furniture, French-style chimney glasses in gilt frames, silk curtains, a 6½ octave Clementi pianoforte, a library of 800 books, pictures and the contents of the wine cellar. This included several bottles of fine old port, Duff Gordon's Sherry, East India Madeira and a quantity of claret wine, old rum and whiskey[28].

Mrs Robertson thereafter lived permanently in the Brighton house with her children.

Sadly, Josepha and Richard's sons died young, both at the age of 29. Richard Maxwell Gordon trained as an agricultural engineer and emigrated firstly to America, and then moved to Australia, where he died in 1866 from alcohol poisoning[29]. Vincent Stuart joined the 2nd Dragoon Guards as a cornet (the lowest rank of commissioned officer in a cavalry troop, equivalent to second lieutenant) and served in India. After a short time he resigned his commission and joined the Bengal Mounted Police. At around the same time he married Mary Augusta Christie Knyvett.

Their marriage was short-lived; the birth of their second child in 1869 was apparently a very difficult one. Their daughter, Margaret Agnes Josepha, had physical disabilities[30] and Mary died shortly after the birth. Vincent brought his two tiny children home from India and left them with his mother in Brighton. He returned to India, and was on his way home again in 1871 when he died at sea, on R.M.S. Windsor Castle. His death certificate states the cause of death to be "paralysis," which probably indicates polio, though "paralysis" and "general paralysis of the insane" were sometimes used to indicate syphilis.

Josepha's two daughters made respectable marriages to clergymen; Josepha Peyton to Rev. Roderick Bain Mackenzie, and Jessie Mary to Rev. Walter Marsham Hoare, a member of the famous banking family.

William Vincent junior (1809-1872) followed his father and grandfather through Westminster School, to becoming a Church of England priest. After graduating from Christ Church College, Oxford, he served parishes in Steventon, Berkshire and Islington, London, before his final appointment in Chipperfield, King's Langley. He and his wife, Ann Stace, had no children.

John Francis (1810-1890) went to Westminster School, but after a short time moved to Felstead School, then joined the East India Seminary at Addiscombe. He joined the army of the East India Company and served in the 23rd Light Infantry, later becoming Lieutenant in the 23rd Madras Native Infantry. On retiring from the army, he lived in Suffolk and was J.P. for the county. John Francis married twice, firstly to Sarah Hingeston and secondly to Rachel Louisa Ward, but had no children.

Frances Ann (1807-1886) married Reginald Brook Boddington, and thus became related to the famous brewing family. They lived in Titley, Herefordshire. Their daughter, Frances Elizabeth Boddington, later settled in Abbey Road, Brighton with her husband, Rev. Charles Smith, within a short walk of her aunt Mrs Robertson in College Place. It's thanks to Frances and Reginald's son, Reginald Stewart Boddington, that there is an extensive genealogy available for the Vincents and their relatives. The family trees he researched and drew up appeared in publications such as *Miscellanea Genealogica et Heraldica* which are freely available online, on sites such as www.archive.org

Worsleys of the Isle of Wight

The Vincents stayed in touch with the family of George Giles' first wife, Mary Worsley. She was a member of the influential family whose name can still be found in many towns of the Isle of Wight. The Worsleys were associated with Appuldurcombe House, Billingham Manor, Gatcombe Park, Chale and Godshill. Mary was one of 16 children of the Rev. Francis Worsley, rector of Chale.

George Giles remarried ten years after Mary's death, but their grandson, Charles Greaves Vincent, would go into the legal business with his older cousin-once-removed, Jonathan Worsley. Charles Greaves settled down in Ryde and took over the legal practice when Jonathan Worsley retired. He became Ryde's town clerk, married a Scottish lady, Jean Bain Gibson, and raised a large family of his own, of one son and eight daughters. Jonathan's brother, Rev. John Henry Worsley, moved to mainland England, where he served in parishes in Tilehurst, west Berkshire and Oxfordshire for most of his clerical career.

Bonnetts of Avington

Emilia's aunt, Louisa Joanna Tappenden, had married the Rev. Charles Shrubsole Bonnett back in 1819, their marriage service led by Rev. William St. Andrew Vincent. The Bonnetts lived a comfortable gentry life, since Mr. Bonnett served for forty years as Rector of Avington, in the beautiful Itchen Valley near Winchester, Hampshire, and for part of that time was also chaplain to the Duke of Buckingham and Chandos, who lived nearby at Avington Park. Like most country parsons, Mr. Bonnett supported his local village school, and was part of the church's efforts to promote wholesome family activities in the community. The social problems caused by excessive alcohol consumption affected most areas, urban and rural, and churches of all denominations organised social activities in the hope of offering an alternative, especially to men, to drinking at the pub.

Mr. Bonnett was especially remembered for encouraging the traditional Maying festival, held annually at Whitsun.[31]

The Bonnetts lived in the village rectory at Avington, near Winchester for forty years, and raised their five children;

Anne Margaret (Annie, Mrs Stephen Terry), 1821-1879

Caroline Louisa, 1823-1887 (later to go into partnership with Emilia Vincent).

Stephen, 1826-1886

Charles Arthur, 1828-1874

Terrys of Dummer

Anne Margaret (Annie) Bonnett married into another family of the landed gentry when the Rev. Stephen Terry became her husband.

Stephen's father, Stephen Terry senior, was a soldier turned gentleman farmer, an enthusiast of county sport, hunting, shooting and fishing, and society events. He'd been a captain of Eton and served with the 62nd Regiment of Militia. He travelled extensively throughout the county, and indeed, most of the country; and as the village of Dummer is about three miles from Steventon, in his younger days he had ample opportunity to dance with his "lively and unassuming neighbour," Jane Austen[32] and went shooting with the Duke of Wellington[33]. The Terrys and Austens were good friends, and both families were delighted when Stephen's son George Seymer Terry married Jane Austen's cousin, Georgiana Lefroy[34].

The Vincents and Tappendens of Westminster met up with the Terrys at least once; in 1851, Stephen Terry recorded in his diary that he went to London to see the Great Exhibition in Hyde Park. On the way, he went to morning prayers at Westminster Abbey, which were led that day by Jenkin Edward Tappenden, and then went to the Tappendens', just a few doors away in Great College Street, for breakfast. After breakfast, his son, Rev. Stephen, and daughter-in-law, Annie, met him there, and they went on to the Great Exhibition together[35].

Stephen Terry senior and Jenkin and Jemima Tappenden were of a similar age; and related by marriage. At some point, the elderly London dwellers may have been advised to spend some time in the country; or perhaps they were invited; or perhaps the London family requested support from the Terrys on their behalf. In any event, they spent their last days at Dummer; Jemima was 68 in 1855, when she died from Erisipelas, a type of cellulitis[36]. Jenkin Edward was 69 when he died from bronchitis the following year[37].

Later, the Terry family fortunes went into decline; Mr. Terry blamed the price of wheat and the cost of maintaining Dummer House. He sold up in 1866, and moved into a property in Weston Patrick, Hampshire, where his son the Rev. Stephen was the vicar[38].

Chapter four: Emilia at home

In 1841, when Emilia was 12, the Westminster Vincents were living in Broad Sanctuary[39], in a house that was adjacent to the arch into Dean's Yard. That house was later demolished, for that side of Dean's Yard to be replaced with George Gilbert Scott's grand gothic-style terrace, now known as The Sanctuary.

Ann Goddard, Elizabeth Bristow, Martha Tolfree and Margaret Roberts were the servants; four female servants indicate a well-off, upper-middle-class family; the class of people who lived comfortably, and whose sons would become clergymen, senior civil servants, lawyers or army officers.

As part of the improvements to Westminster Abbey's surroundings, a new house was planned for the Chapter Clerk; in due course, Emilia and her family moved into 21 Dean's Yard. This brand-new house had up-to-date facilities, including piped water, which would have saved the servants many trips a day to the pump in Dean's Yard. The house incorporated a passageway through to Mr. Vincent's office, which was where the present-day Westminster Abbey gift shop stands.

There may have been more than a touch of nepotism in Mr. Vincent's appointment as Chapter Clerk, since he was appointed at the time his father was Dean of Westminster. However, as a solicitor and conveyancer, he was at least qualified for the role, and seems to have been methodical and conscientious.

He took his responsibility as registrar for the Abbey seriously; when he took office in 1803, he found the Abbey registers in disorder. In June 1804, he had *"ordered that Mr. Horsfall make up the Register Book of Burials to the time of Mr. Vincent's appointment to the office of Chapter Clerk, and, that Mr. Horsfall be allowed one month from this day to make up the said book, and if*

it be not made up at that day, Mr. Vincent be authorised
to employ some person to make it up, upon such evidence
as is still in existence[40]."

A property expert, he was part of the Dean and
Chapter's decision to pull down some dilapidated houses
at the front of Dean's Yard, on the grounds of opening up
the vista of the abbey, and then, more controversially, the
decision to replace them with newer buildings on
virtually the same footprint. This was George Gilbert
Scott's grand neo-gothic terrace, The Sanctuary, which is
now occupied by businesses.

Over the years, George Giles Vincent built up his own
portfolio of property, which included land, houses and
interests in Wheal Vincent (later Altarnun Consols) a tin
mining enterprise near Launceston, Cornwall[41].

Life at the Abbey would have exposed Emilia and her
siblings to every section of society. Living on Dean's Yard
meant daily contact with the boys who streamed in and
out of Westminster School and used Dean's Yard as a
playground and assembly point. There were regular fist
fights in Dean's Yard (known as Green), between boys of
the school, or between boys and passers-by who had the
temerity to intercept a football that went over the
railings.

Their neighbours in the abbey community were an
interesting mix of aristocratic, religious, legal and
creative people; Lord and Lady John Thynne; the Deans
of Westminster, Drs. Ireland, Turton, Trench, Buckland
and Stanley; the Milmans; Mr. James Turle the abbey
organist and his large family; Reptons and Freres, Mr.
Liddell, the father of Alice; Canon Dr. Christopher
Wordsworth, nephew of the poet.

Figure 4; 21 Dean's Yard in October 2010.
Photo by Tony Hisgett, Flickr

Emilia's father, George Giles Vincent comes across as principled and generous. He gave money to support projects for the poor, including supporting the daughter of a Dean's Yard neighbour, Rev. James W. Dodd. Mr. Dodd had been an usher (master) at Westminster School for more 30 years, until he died in 1818. He had four daughters, one of whom was widowed around 1840 and left in straitened circumstances. Mr. Dodd's friends rallied to her support; even taking out an advertisement in *The Times* to ask for contributions. The name of George Giles Vincent was on the list of contributors[42].

As Chapter Clerk, he was part of the discussions of the Dean and Chapter of Westminster to demolish the slums and rebuild the area. Like many, the juxtaposition of rich and poor, and the wretched situation of the latter, vexed him.

His brother-in-law, Jenkin Edward Tappenden would sometimes tell the story of the time he was walking along the New Road, when a young hoodlum picked his pocket, relieving him of a handkerchief worth five shillings. He took the youth into custody himself, delivering him to Police Constable Dennis Keays, who searched him, and found the handkerchief in his pocket. Henry Brown, aged 19, was tried at the Old Bailey in April 1833, found guilty and sentenced to transportation for 14 years. Six weeks later, he was on his way to Van Dieman's Land (Tasmania) on the convict ship *Stakesby*.[43]

Was there a better way to deal with the crimes driven by poverty? Could young people be educated into better ways? Was it right to have a society where so many people struggled to make ends meet, on wages of eight to ten shillings a week, while others could own a handkerchief worth five shillings? Could it be true that God had ordained the situations of both rich and poor, and both should accept both their station in life, and the responsibility to do their best with it? These may well have been matters of debate in this well-off, and conscientious family.

Mr. Vincent worked as a solicitor all his adult life, and for the Dean and Chapter of Westminster for most of it, but also studied philosophy and wrote several books exploring morals and ethics, which show familiarity with the works of John Locke, David Hume, Thomas Hobbes and William Paley, and (perhaps unsurprisingly for a man of the law), the Commentaries on the Laws of England compiled by Sir William Blackstone. His writings reveal a man concerned with justice and doing the right thing.

His Christian faith was integral; in his first work, *An Explanation of Morality and of Good and Evil; or the Laws and Rules of Human Actions generally,* published in 1823, he posited a three-fold scriptural base for morality;

From Matthew 12:12, where Jesus points out the lawfulness of rescuing an animal from a pit on the Sabbath, he draws the principle that laws are for human benefit, and not for their own sake.

From Matthew 22:39, *"Thou shalt love thy neighbour as thyself,"* comes the principle that morality is a communal, not a personal thing only.

Lastly, from Matthew 5:39-40, where Jesus recommends not responding in kind to evil acts, Mr. Vincent draws the principle that people should endeavour to return good for evil wherever possible, rather than *"be unrelenting and resentful[44]."*

He was an old-fashioned gentleman; he believed in his responsibility to provide for and protect the women in his life, and was horrified by *"... rites among other nations and people, of self-immolation and destruction; and those of the sacrifice or destruction of females and female children; and of that deplorable custom of infanticide[45]."*

George Giles Vincent believed that liberty was a fundamental human right; but at the same time, the abolition of black slavery was not a straightforward issue for him. Black faces were known to Londoners; a Dean's Yard neighbour, Rev. Stephen Rigaud, had a black butler in 1848[46].

But Mr. Vincent had grown up in an era of slavery, and lived in a society that had grown prosperous from the labour of black slaves.

Figure 5; George Giles Vincent (1774-1859). Copyright: Dean and Chapter of Westminster

In 1807, the UK parliament had passed the Slave Trade Act, which outlawed the trading of slaves, but this did not end the captivity of those already in slavery.

His writings play out the unease of contemporary discussions on the subject. He realised there would be political and social upheavals, if estates and colonies were abandoned, along with the common concern that a likely alternative to enslaving captives of war would be killing them; *"the effusion of human blood [might be] spared by affording a mart for captives among barbarous and uncivilised nations and people*[47].*"*

Moreover, the Vincents had relatives who had directly benefited from enslaved labour.

In 1833, the Slavery Abolition Law was passed, and resulted in the British government raising loans of £20m to purchase the freedom of slaves in the Caribbean and Africa; in the same year, Emilia's cousin, Josepha Mary, married Richard Robertson, an accountant at the Metropolitan Board of Roads, and also the private secretary of the Postmaster General, Lord Lowther. His uncle, also called Richard Robertson, had served as a member of the ruling council of the Caribbean island of St. Vincent's, and owned the Struan Cottage plantation there. The emancipation of his slaves cost the British government £2,231 3s 10d [48].

In 1843, Mr. Robertson senior caused something of a scandal when he brought his mistress, Eliza Dempster, a former black slave, to London and married her (which may or may not show that he regarded her as an equal)[49].

Chapter five: Education

When it came to education, Victorian boys and girls were treated very differently.

Emilia's brothers, George and Thomas, attended Westminster school, the almer mater of their father, uncle, grandfather and numerous other male relatives. George then became a solicitor and was appointed as Steward of the Manors of Westminster. Francis does not appear in the available school lists, so perhaps was educated at home or sent to a private tutor. Thomas went from Westminster School to St. John's College, Cambridge[50] and became a priest.

There is no record of the education Hannah, Mary and Emilia received, but as a wealthy family, they had choices. It's possible that they were sent to school; there were many fee-paying schools in London, including for girls. Small schools for all classes abounded; quality varied dramatically, and parents tended to get what they could pay for.

If Mrs Vincent were interested in educating her daughters, she may have taught them herself; or as Hannah was so much older than her sisters, she may have taken charge of their education.

A common option for families of the Vincents' wealth was to employ a governess at home. The typical governess was a woman of similar social class, unmarried or widowed, who needed to earn a living, and would have had few other options for respectable employment. Some families, if they wished their girls to learn a foreign language, would employ a governess of the desired nationality. The 1841 census, when Emilia was 12, does not include a governess, but this might simply mean that the census, which always covers a Sunday night, coincided with the governess' night off. Besides, governesses did not necessarily live in.

In central Westminster, a governess would not be hard to find. Recommendations were often by word of mouth, and a family who no longer needed a governess would usually help her to find her next position. There were also governess agencies, such as Mrs Smith's of Alfred Place, Bedford Square[51], or Mrs Hinton's of Soho Square[52], and use of such an agency may have ensured some level of quality. Both Mrs Smith's and Mrs Hinton's newspaper advertisements promise to match families with suitable governesses, English or foreign, at varying levels of experience and cost.

If the Vincents did not employ a governess or send their daughters to school, they may have sent them to a private tutor, and with so many clergymen and their wives around Dean's Yard, they would have had plenty to choose from. Not all clergymen had a private income as well as a church stipend; it was both common and acceptable for clergymen, or their wives, to take in pupils to earn extra income, either on a daily or a boarding basis.

The small school at Bloomsbury which advertised in the Morning Herald in 1840 may have been one of the better ones, since it mentions all the accomplishments expected of a lady and little that would prepare one for the world of everyday work;

"SUPERIOR EDUCATION FOR SIX YOUNG LADIES in a clergyman's family, where the lady devotes herself with maternal solicitude to the comfort and best interests of her pupils, assisted by first-rate masters for the harp, pianoforte, singing, drawing, dancing, French, Italian, Greek, Latin, use of globes and moral philosophy... in a

> *pleasant and healthy village, four miles*
> *from London. Terms 60 guineas per*
> *annum, which includes all the above-*
> *named branches of education[53]."*

The quality of the education received by Hannah, Mary and Emilia Vincent is impossible to judge, as there were no qualifications needed to become a governess or private tutor.

A girl might be taught the classics, Latin, modern languages, mathematics and science by an intelligent and educated governess or tutor, and so receive an education not much different from her brothers at school. She was probably more likely to receive the basic accomplishments she would need for the life of a wife and mother; she would one day be managing a large household and would need skills of reading and writing, arithmetic for recording household accounts, drawing, needlework and embroidery to keep her occupied, knitting so that she could make warm garments for the poor, music and singing so that she could be a good hostess for her husband's guests. No doubt Hannah, Margaret and Emilia were encouraged to view their brothers' friends from Westminster School as potential husbands, and may have looked forward to being the wives of doctors, lawyers, military officers or clergymen.

One of the Vincents' neighbours, Rev. Temple Frere, sent at least one of his sons to a small school for 34 boys run by Rev. Mr. Furlong at his rectory at Warfield, Berkshire.

Warfield then was a quiet farming village, in between the Thames and the market town of Bracknell. This quiet community was shocked by the tragic events of a night in March 1839, when the school and rectory were destroyed by a fire, which started in a closet in the butler's pantry. It seems that 11-year-old Griffith Temple Frere was one of the first to discover the fire; the household scrambled to evacuate, with the rector, his servants and his older children battling through the smoke to awaken all the children and lead them outside. But when the roll was called outside, Griffith was missing, and it was speculated later that he had gone back inside to retrieve his clothing.

A little later Griffith was seen at a window, and Mr. Furlong ran to fetch a ladder, only to find it was too short to reach the window. Mr. Furlong tried to reach Griffith anyway, but fell from the ladder. He tried again, and this time Griffith appeared at the window, and managed to smash the glass himself. The boy put out a leg, but then fell back out of sight and was not seen alive again.

Everything was lost; the servants had not even saved their shoes; the rural nature of the area meant that there was hardly anyone who could help. Their nearest neighbour, Miss Terry, was away from home, but her servants turned out to do what they could, including to run further afield for help.

Lady Malcolm and the Misses Malcolm ran the mile from Warfield Place and assisted in the rescue. Lady Malcolm sent a servant to Windsor, but it took an hour and a half to return with two engines and a troop of the Blues. It was too late; Mr. Furlong, his family, pupils and servants were left homeless. His friends and the neighbouring clergy were generous in their support; Mrs Furlong and her small children, with 10 of the pupils, went to Lady Malcolm's; 10 more went to Lady Wilder at Binfield Manor House; others went to the Rev. J. Randall's, at Binfield, the Rev. Townsend's at Easthampstead, and to Miss Terry's, until their parents could be contacted[54].

In modern times, a school premises would have a full set of risk assessments, in which the lack of means of escape, the lack of an alarm system, and the distance from the nearest fire brigade would be items of concern. But in March 1839, an inquest on the death of 11-year-old Griffith Temple Frere was held at the school and the jury returned a verdict of "accidental death.[55]"

Westminster School

James Tappenden had sent his boys to Rugby[56]; but the Westminster branch of the family did not waste its close proximity to Westminster School, where Dean William Vincent had been usher and Headmaster. He had sent his sons, George Giles and William St. Andrew there, where their school fellows, typically the sons of well-off merchants, Members of Parliament, and the landed classes, were bound for the church, the armed forces, politics or the law. William St. Andrew had been a King's Scholar, a scholarship that would have saved his family around £60 per year in fees.

In those days, boarding was not fully integrated into school life, and those boys who were not day boys had to be separately booked into one of the nearby boarding houses; these were run as independent businesses by a succession of house masters and mistresses.

George and William, though, would have merely walked across the yard from their home, the headmaster's house, since they enjoyed the privilege – or otherwise – of being taught by their father. Their sons in turn arrived at the school well after Mr. Vincent had safely moved to the Deanery.

There is no record of Emilia's middle brother, Francis, in the school lists; he may have gone to another school, or was perhaps not well during childhood, and not considered fit enough to cope with the rough and tumble of public-school life. If that was the case, he may have been educated at home with his sisters or sent to a private tutor; he still acquired enough education to secure a position at the Office of Wood and Works.

Like most public schools of the time, Westminster taught mostly Latin and Greek, and had a system of fagging, whereby younger boys acted as servants for older boys. Corporal punishment was used enthusiastically.

Standards would seem primitive by today's standards;

The memoirs of former pupils speak of the boys' habit of breaking windows in the summer to relieve the unbearable heat, since many of the windows could not be opened. Then in winter, the room literally froze, part of the floor becoming an ice slide[57].

Some of the boys had to perform their ablutions in a stone trough, "foul with the mould of time[58]" in a washroom, known as "the way," which had the interesting feature of being flushed through by the river Thames at high tide. In the overcrowded boarding houses around Dean's Yard, there was a lack of basic furniture and even basic housekeeping. At the time when the school was full, the boys were crammed together, *"higgledy-piggledy, side by side and topsy turvey like pigs in a sty. There they were, some blacking shoes, others cooking mutton chops, others boiling coffee, all in one room together[59]."*

One day, Lady Mansfield visited her son, who was ill. She found him sitting in the only chair in the room, with a friend sitting on the coal scuttle; whereupon the friend politely got up and offered the coal scuttle to Lady Mansfield[60].

Arthur Stanley, who was Dean of Westminster from 1864, recalled travelling to Oxford with William Buckland, who had become Dean in 1845. Buckland had been shocked at the conditions he found at Westminster school. Perhaps, though, Mr. Stanley's friend had been exaggerating when he said the counterpanes in the dormitory had not been washed for 11 years and the school had not been cleaned since the days of Elizabeth[61].

Buckland's daughter, Mrs Gordon, in her biography of her father, confirms that the college *dormitory "was in a most dismal condition; with the walls blackened by smoke, and here and there, hung with moth-eaten green baise curtains; the tables and lockers seamed and scarred in all directions... The floor was only cleaned once a year[62]."*

There had been a history of funding issues; before the Public School Act of 1862, the Dean and Chapter of Westminster was responsible for the upkeep of the school, but was not always willing to spend what was necessary to keep the buildings in good order, since the funds would come from the incomes of the officers of the Dean and Chapter. At the same time, other prestigious schools such as Eton and Winchester were perceived as having more pleasant and healthier surroundings; the expansion of the city meant that Westminster had become further and further away from the countryside.

Westminster School did retain the loyalty of some old boys, including George Giles and William St. Andrew Vincent, who continued to send their sons, but the school declined in popularity and numbers. In 1827, there were 254 pupils. By 1841, there were only 60[63]; the Vincent boys probably counted themselves lucky that at least they did not have to board there, and could enjoy home comforts.

In 1846, a new broom, Rev. Henry George Liddell, swept in. In a break with tradition, his appointment was deliberately that of a non-Old Westminster so that there was no danger of nostalgia and sentiment in his decision-making. Mr. Liddell and Dean Buckland are credited with driving through the structural improvements necessary to raise standards and restore confidence in the school.

Mr. Liddell, his wife, Lorina, and their family moved into the headmaster's house. In 1852, their fourth child, Alice Pleasance Liddell was born – the Alice who is famous for being Lewis Carroll's friend and inspiration. Emilia is certain to have been aware of the young Alice; the headmaster and his family would have been within the same social circle within the community of Westminster Abbey. How much Alice was aware of Emilia, though, is another matter, since she was only four years old when the Liddells left the abbey community for Oxford, where Mr. Liddell became Dean of Christ Church.

Emilia's brothers went into the expected respectable professions; George followed his father into the law. Francis became a civil servant at the Office of Wood and Works. Thomas went to St. John's College, Oxford, and then followed their grandfather and uncle into the church.

Chapter six: The Coronation of Queen Victoria

The first major public event of Emilia's life happened in June 1838, when she was almost 10 years old.

The death of King William IV the previous year meant that there was a new young Queen, and Westminster Abbey was at the centre of the empire's attention as preparations began for the coronation. George Giles Vincent, Emilia's father, as Chapter Clerk of Westminster Abbey, would have been heavily involved with the Abbey's preparations for the momentous event; along with the Clerk of Works, who oversaw the ambitious construction work, and the Duke of Norfolk, who was busy with the administration.

As a child of nine, Emilia was surely caught up with the excitement of the great occasion. She would have observed the preparations going on in and around the abbey, much of it under the direction of principal carpenter, James Ratcliffe; from the first wagonload of timber arriving at the great doors, the rattling and banging of scaffolding, and the building of the tiered galleries that would protect the monuments from damage and eventually seat 7,000 spectators, plus 400 or so musicians, choristers and officiants; then the construction of a gothic-style reception suite by the west door.

Then after the building work, the decorations. The abbey was transformed from its usual dark edifice full of tombs and monuments into a lavish theatre with hangings of rich fabrics in scarlet and purple with gold trimmings, coats of arms, and extra lights.

As reported in The Globe,

"One thing which strikes the spectator immediately on entering the galleries is, that nothing of the monuments in this splendid edifice is visible; they have been carefully

covered from sight, and every precaution seems to have been taken to guard them, as well as every part of the building, from injury.[64]"

Although Emilia was no doubt forbidden from entering the Abbey while construction was going on, perhaps she and her friends played some lovely games in the cavernous spaces created by the erection of the banks of seating; spaces that would be furnished with long tables for serving refreshments.

Perhaps she was aware of the jostling for tickets, and the complaints as even the richest families in the realm could not obtain more tickets than their quota.

In front of the west door, the temporary gothic style portico was designed to blend in with the Abbey itself, beautifully furnished and carpeted, with rooms either side for the reception of the Queen and her royal relatives.

The whole of the capital was gearing up for celebration; the surrounding streets were being festooned with banners and bunting, and gas-lit illuminations were appearing on the surrounding public buildings. A huge fair was being set up in Hyde Park and all along the streets along the procession route, anyone who owned a house or even a tiny piece of land was building a bank of seating on it and selling tickets. Seats at prime positions near the abbey were being sold for as much as two guineas[65].

Mr. Vincent, like his neighbours, hoped to make a little money out of the occasion. For the coronation of Victoria's uncle, King George IV in 1821, Mr. Vincent had rented out the space in front of his own house in Broad Sanctuary to two builders, who erected a bank of seating; on the condition that they did not obscure the view from his own windows. He also allowed ladies using the stand to walk through his house to use the privy[66]. He may well have done the same in 1831 and 1838.

Coronation music

In many areas, the organisers at the 1838 coronation were anxious not to repeat the mistakes of the last; William IV, mindful of his late brother, George IV's, much criticised extravagance in 1821, had wanted to set an example of royal prudence; but went too far and his coronation had been criticised for being cheap and shabby.

The new Queen wanted to steer a middle path, with a coronation that was neither too lavish nor too cheap, and this included the provision of music for the ceremony itself. During the preparations, normal services of the abbey were much disrupted. Walter Macfarren, an Abbey chorister, later wrote;

"...the choir was, for many months, completely dismantled, and divine service, during this protracted period, was held only on Sundays and Saints' days, in Henry VII's Chapel, and this circumstance led to a large number of holidays. There was no organ in that historic chapel, and I well remember that the late James Turle gave us our key on an old fashioned and cumbrous pitchpipe.[67]"

At King William's coronation, the orchestra in the Abbey had contained just 187 performers, which was assessed to be too small a number to give full effect to choral music in that large space. For Victoria, the orchestra would comprise 400 performers. The abbey organ would be dismantled and temporarily replaced by an organ especially built by Messrs Hill and Davison, the first English organ to be built to the CC manual compass[68]. It would be placed much further back and connected by a long movement with the keys in front of the orchestra[69]. From this position, the organist, Sir George Smart, had Mr. Kramer, the orchestra leader, and the whole body of instrumentalists in his view, and he would perform the role of orchestra director as well as play the new organ. However, it was much debated in the musical press as to whether Sir George could be successful in this dual role.

Why not use the services of Mr. James Turle, who was, after all, organist of Westminster Abbey and the regular leader of the abbey choir? But Sir George, as senior organist at the Chapel Royal, took precedence; and he had performed the dual role, as organist and director of the orchestra, at the coronation of William IV. But this time, it was a much larger orchestra and choir to direct, plus a more complicated organ.

Mr. Turle had supporters at *"The Musical World."*

The writer considered that it would be *"an act of injustice towards a most worthy and talented member of the profession* [Mr. Turle], *and exhibiting a shameless disregard of the proprietaries of a musical solemnities. We allude to the music director undertaking the diametrically opposed offices of conducting a crowded orchestra, and performing on a large German organ with two octaves of pedals. We presume the most talented organist in Europe, whoever that individual may be, never dreamt of such a combination of duties in his most ambitious moments.[70]"*

The publication went so far as to suggest that Sir George Smart's motives might be influenced by the fact that as organist, he would be paid a fee of between £200 and £300, whereas the role of conductor on its own would merely enhance his reputation[71].

In the event, Mr. Turle accepted a face-saving solution; he sang in the choir.

At the next coronation, that of Edward VII in 1902, the roles of organist and musical director were separated.

Coronation music rehearsal

The day before the coronation itself, an orderly and good-natured crowd gathered at the Poet's Corner entrance to attend the grand rehearsal of the coronation music.

The top-priced tickets were for the gallery erected for the members of the House of Commons, with cheaper seats available in the triforium; the highest level of Westminster Abbey. It was obvious that this was a rehearsal; carpenters and upholsterers continued to work, and sometimes succeeded in keeping their actions quiet. There were pauses to give out music, shout out instructions and long waits between items. The Bishop of London was trying out the pulpit.

The *Morning Advertiser* described the scene;

"Sir George Smart appeared in front of the choir, put his hands to his mouth, and bawled at the top of his voice to the opposite aisle, "Are the trumpets ready?" making the walls of the Abbey reverberate with the sound; the trumpeters, however, did not hear.

Sir George Smart again called out, "Are you ready with your trumpets, Mr. Harper?"

"Yes," answered Mr. Harper, and immediately there was a splendid flourish of trumpets.

"Now for God save the queen," said Sir George.

After the national anthem, Sir George Smart called for another grand flourish, and Mr. Harper's trumpeters obliged.

"Exceedingly well, Mr. Harper," called Sir George[72]".

The orchestra included Nicolas Mori, the famous violinist, cellist Robert Lindley, and Domenico Dragonetti, whose three-stringed double-bass had been especially made for him, because of his unusual height.

The *Morning Advertiser* continued;

"...After waiting a little while during the call of the roll for the distribution of the music amongst the members of the choir, and an inconsiderably great while for no apparent purpose at all, for Lindley had thrice taken the accustomed pinch of snuff to which he treats himself 'ere he commences any great undertaking, and Mori had half a dozen times tried his violin, and old Dragonetti had fairly gone to sleep with his ponderous instrument reposing on his bosom, and the flutists furtively blew, but Sir George was imperturbable; at length the mighty hand of the conductor was raised, and off went the choir as one instrument and one voice[73]."

The choir consisted of members of several choirs, including from the Chapel Royal, and the Abbey itself, augmented by professional and amateur singers. If Emilia's brother Thomas were in the choir, he would have been singing with the adults, since he was in his last year at Westminster School. If not with the choir, he may have been in another set of seats reserved for Westminster boys, because the Queen's Scholars at that time had a right of admission to all major events[74].

At the centre of it all was the spot where the ceremony was to take place, and the 19-year-old Princess Alexandrina Victoria of Kent would be crowned Queen of the United Kingdom of Great Britain and Northern Ireland. Overhead, was a small door where a man was stationed to communicate the exact moment when the crown was placed on her head. He would give a signal to the semaphore at the Admiralty, from where the signal would be transmitted elsewhere. This would trigger a double royal salute of 41 guns, with the response from the guns of the Tower of London, Windsor, Woolwich, and elsewhere[75].

If Emilia's parents were in the abbey, and her brother Thomas sitting with the Westminster boys, or in the choir, Emilia herself was likely to be at home, with the servants and any other family members not able to get a seat in the abbey.

The excitement of this major event was tinged with sadness; Emilia's grandmother, Margaret Tappenden, a frail old lady of 86, had died that week. But any family members who attended the ceremony had to suspend their mourning for the duration; no mourning clothes were allowed in the Abbey. Ladies were dressed in their most colourful finery; some in court clothes, some in evening dresses. As the newspaper *Bell's Life in London* described,

"The effect was extremely grand; the beautiful admixture of white satin, crimson velvet, tipped and dotted in all directions by the brilliant head dresses which their ladyships wore, and all this in motion, it was like a scene from fairyland, or some gorgeous bird rattling its rich plumage in the sunlight[76]."

The Vincent family at home, dressed in mourning black, would nonetheless be unable to resist watching from an upper window, perhaps following the order of the procession as published by the London newspapers and working out who was who amongst the foreign ambassadors, regiments of troops, bandsmen and British nobles.

From their vantage point overlooking Broad Sanctuary, they could witness the colourful entourage. The procession was in strict order; trumpeters led the way, followed by a squadron of Life Guards. Then came the carriages of foreign ambassadors, followed by mounted bands of Household Brigades. A detachment of

Life Guards accompanied each of the carriages of the royal family, in order of precedence; first, the Duchess of Kent, the Queen's mother. After her, the Duchess of Gloucester, the Duke and Duchess of Cambridge, and the Duke of Sussex.

At last, the queen's party of twelve carriages arrived, with escorts, ladies-in-waiting, gentleman ushers and grooms, with Yeoman of the Guards riding or walking alongside. Finally, the state coach, drawn by eight cream-coloured horses, attended by a Yeoman of the Guard at each wheel, and two footmen at each door, and followed by a final squadron of Life Guards[77].

Sir George Webbe Dasent, who attended Westminster School 1830-1834, included many interesting details about school life in his autobiography, *Annals of an Eventful Life,* (published in three volumes) and his semi-autobiographical novel *Half a Life* (published in two volumes). He describes his character's presence in the Abbey for the coronation of William IV in 1831. He noted that seating had been installed in the triforium — Westminster Abbey's attic.

The triforium of Westminster Abbey today has been transformed into a modern museum, with a new tower accommodating an elevator. But in Emilia's day, most of the time, it was a dusty attic with rough floors and used as a storage place for old monuments, spare waxworks and random storage chests. It was accessed from a steep and narrow staircase adjacent to Poets Corner.

Figure 6; The triforium, drawing by Herbert Railton

For coronations, though, this extra space, with its overhead view of the nave of the abbey, became an extra seating area. Dasent described a refreshment stand, a rather expensive one. In one scene, he describes how a kindly, elderly peer bought his character some food, and the stall holder refused to give him change from a sovereign (£1)[78], which would have made those refreshments very expensive indeed.

Arthur Penrhyn Stanley, a son of the Bishop of Norwich, was 23 in 1838, and he too watched the coronation service from the triforium. He later married one of the Queen's ladies-in-waiting, Lady Augusta Bruce, and became Dean of Westminster in 1864. He wrote of the coronation to a friend on 4 July 1838;

"At 5:30 [am] *we started; London all awake; the streets crowded. At 7:00* [am] *we reached the Abbey. My mother and sister were deposited behind the peeresses and I was taken up to the vaultings* [the triforium] *to my brother and sister. This was the first view of the Abbey I had – most glorious, the dazzling splendour of the prodigious crowd all in their full dress, and literally "living out" upon the walls. I ... saw everything but the nave* [he probably means the transept] *and peeresses, being very high up, but with the widest possible view.*

It was perfectly easy to walk about in the hinder and therefore unoccupied parts of the gallery, where were refreshments &c. prepared, with the most perfect convenience. At 9 the guns announced that the queen had left the palace; an electric shock ran visibly through the whole Abbey, and from that time till the end of it all, at 3:30, the interest was so intense that I did not feel exhausted for a moment. At 10:30 another gun announced that she was at the abbey door, and in about a quarter of an hour the procession appeared from under the organ, advancing up the purple approach to the chancel – everyone leaning over – and in they came: first the great Dukes struggling with the enormous trains; then bishops &c ; and then the queen with her vast crimson train, outspread by eight ladies all in white, followed by the great ladies of her court in enormous crimson trains, and the smaller ladies, with delicate sky blue trains, trailing along the dark floor.

When she came within the full view of the gorgeous Abbey, she paused, as if for breath, and clasped her hands. The orchestra broke out into the most tremendous crash of music I ever heard.

"I was glad when they said unto me, let us go into the house of the Lord."

Everyone literally gasped for breath from the intense interest, and the rails of the gallery visibly trembled in

*one's hands from the trembling of the spectators. I never
saw anything like it; tears would have been a relief; one
felt that the queen must sink into the earth under the
tremendous awe. But at last she moved on to her place
by the altar, and (as I heard from one of my cousins who
had a place close by) threw herself on her knees, buried
her face in her hands, and evidently prayed fervently.
For the first part the silence was so great that at my
extreme point I could hear quite distinctly the tremulous
but articulate voice of the Archbishop; afterwards it was
quite inaudible...*

*The very moment the crown touched her head the guns
went off - the trumpets began, and the shouts; she was
perfectly immovable, like a statue. The Duchess of Kent
burst into tears, and her lady had to put on her coronet
for her. The anointing was very beautiful from the cloth
of gold; the homage also, from the magnificent cluster in
the very centre...*

*All the movements were beautiful. She was always
accompanied by her eight ladies, floating about her like a
silvery cloud. It was over at 3:30. She went out then
with her crown, her orb, and her sceptre. I walked home;
the rest had to wait till eight for their carriage, which
was forced back by the length of the line to Kennington
Common; the crowd in the streets to see the return of the
procession was stupendous. It was all more like a dream
than a reality – more beautiful than I could have
conceived possible. I should wish almost never to see her
again; that, as this was the first image I have ever had of
her, so it should be the last[79]."*

That evening, nearly every government building
blazed with colourful gas-lit illuminations. Somerset
House displayed a superb bulging imperial crown around
12 feet high, illuminated with gas and variegated lamps
reflected on gold, with stars and the cross of England. At
the Horse Guards, the Royal Standard was floating from

the cupola. At the Ordnance Office in Pall Mall, the whole front of the building was lit up and at the Admiralty was a large imperial crown with two stars. The Home Office illumination was a crown bearing the royal initials, V.R., in gold encircled by a wreath of laurel and palm leaves. At the Colonial office was the inscription "Victoria Regina" formed in jets of gas. There were also illuminations at East India House, Custom House, Excise Office, the Mansion House, the Bank of England, the Guildhall, the General Post Office, Goldsmiths' Hall, Mercers' hall and other civic buildings.[80]

The festivities continued for several more days.

The next day, the galleries of the abbey filled with a new audience for a concert in which the coronation music was played once more.

At Vauxhall pleasure gardens, a grand coronation gala included the intrepid aeronaut, Mr. Green, demonstrating his hot-air "Nassau Balloon[81]".

In Hyde Park, the spectacular fairground covered about 50 acres, and accommodated nearly a thousand temporary theatres, booths and "taverns of every grade[82]." Gambling was strictly forbidden, but there was entertainment of nearly every kind; swingboats, clowns, acrobats and food and drink stalls[83]. The fair was opened by three strokes of a sonorous East Indian gong sounded at the theatrical booth of Johnson and Lee, which was the signal for the musical bands at the various places of amusement to strike up "God save the queen," followed by a simultaneous shout from the congregated multitude[84]. A pyrotechnic show exploded from a huge gallery[85].

In spite of the huge number of tourists in London that week, the police felt that the crowds were mostly good-natured and orderly. However, among the incidents reported was a dispute at the Hyde Park fair, which escalated to an attack by a mob of about 40 people on the owner of a large swing, which consisted of a set of aerial sailing ships. The owner managed to escape out of a back window of his temporary structure, but the mob then set fire to the sails of his vessels. There was another fire at the gingerbread stall belonging to Mr. Potter of Croydon. Mrs Potter made a valiant attempt to put out the flames, but she suffered severe burns in the process, and the stall was destroyed[86].

Police Superintendent Mallalieu later reported that 20 people were arrested that day; one for an old offence, seven who were charged with picking pockets, and the remaining 12 with illegal gambling. Police officers had supervised the area around the pyrotechnics show, and no accidents had occurred there. One man had died at the fair from natural causes, and his body had been conveyed to the workhouse at Saint George's, Hanover Square. The police had also dealt with around 100 lost children[87].

At length, the excitement died down. Workmen returned to Westminster Abbey to dismantle the theatre and reveal the memorials once more. The Hyde Park fair was packed away and removed. The decorated streets returned to normality and the abbey to its everyday calm.

Chapter seven: Sickness and health

The Infirmarer's Garden

In the days when there were Benedictine monks at Westminster, and Dean's Yard was enclosed by a wall and known as "The Elms," and a stream ran through to turn the Abbey mill and pass through to the Thames, there was a miniature monastery within the monastery; a tiny chapel with a cloister and its own little garden[88]. This was the infirmary; the place of retreat for ill or elderly monks. In this little oasis, they had their own replica of abbey life, plus hot baths, a reduced workload, and the care and companionship of their peers.

Black-clad monks tended fruit trees, flowers and medicinal herbs, and at the hours of prayer, their chants mingled with the humming of bees from the hives.

The infirmary church, St. Catherine's chapel, was built with an extra-long nave, designed so that elderly and sick monks could hear the services from their beds in the adjoining hall. Later, the monks wanted more comfortable, individual accommodation with their own fireplaces, and some small houses were built.

Those able to walk just a little further from the cloister could go to the Infirmary Garden, now named College Garden, which at one time had two ponds, stocked with fish and water-lilies. There were fruit trees, herbs and vegetables. There were remedies for cleansing, purging, drawing out and relaxing, flowers and fruit grown for colour and aroma, flavour and texture, income and nourishment. Apples and pears grew in the small orchard, along with medlars which would last through the winter.

Those were the days when bad humours had to be drawn out of the body by bleeding, purging or micturition; the apothecary would advise which one was needed.

A short walk across the stream via Queen Maud's bridge would lead to the mill that stood near the junction of College Street and Millbank Street.

By the time Emilia Vincent lived in Dean's Yard, there were no ponds, no beehives and no mill. Fruit trees had been replaced by planes and other trees, and the garden was a peaceful space for the abbey residents. College Garden was closed to Westminster schoolboys for most of the year; Queen's Scholars were allowed to use the space for three days of sports at the end of term[89].

Since the Reformation, black-clad Anglican clergy had replaced the monks living around the cloisters, but the gardens still represented a place of beauty and calm amid the increasingly noisy city; its vivid hues contrasting with the soot-blackened stones of the Abbey, and summer scents perhaps mitigating the stench of the Thames a little.

Figure 7; College Garden, March 2018. Photo by Colin Tame

Throughout Emilia's lifetime, medicine was progressing; scientific method was being applied, and exciting new theories, such as Germ Theory, were tested. Even so, many physicians relied on what they felt were tried and trusted remedies; including bleeding, alcohol and a stay in the country, as we shall see.

Emilia's motives, in deciding to spend her life caring for others can only be guessed at, but several factors may have contributed to her being drawn in that direction.

Victorian children tended to be aware of sickness and death from a very early age; any family of any class was aware that life was fragile and unpredictable.

It was possible to live into old age – Emilia's grandfather, James Tappenden, lived to be 99 – yet so many babies did not last a year. While some women produced baby after baby for many years, many others did not survive their first confinement. Diseases such as cholera, measles, typhus, diphtheria, polio, and smallpox visited periodically and wrenched away their victims in a matter of days, or even hours. The dreaded consumption (phthisis or tuberculosis) took hold slowly and sucked the life out of sufferers, sometimes over several years. Someone might survive a nasty accident only to die from an infection in the wound. There was no effective treatment for depression, and therefore a high rate of suicide. Health and safety was all but unknown, and left to "common sense" – there was therefore a high level of accidents, for instance, the catastrophic school fire that took the life of Dean's Yard neighbour, Griffith Temple Frere.

If medicine was rudimentary, surgery was worse. There were glaring class differences; a sick person could send for a doctor if they could pay them and buy what they recommended, whether that be a stay in the country, particular food, a medicinal dose of brandy or a special preparation from the apothecary.

Better off people had more space in better housing and cleaner water – or could have water delivered from cleaner areas – more variety of food and access to healthcare. The latter could be regarded, with hindsight, as a mixed blessing. Calling a physician was likely to result in remedies such as bleeding, leeches or cupping followed by a glass of wine, perhaps with opium in it. Surgery was bloody, without anaesthetic and unhygienic; many patients survived the operation only to die from a subsequent infection. Pain relief was available; but opium, frequently in the mixture with alcohol known as laudanum, was highly addictive. In the latter half of the 19th century, more options became available; salicine or salicylic acid, would develop into aspirin, and acetanilide and phenacetin into paracetamol. These could have unpleasant side-effects, but were of some help until the safer formulations were available a few years later.

When someone was ill, there was usually little to be done, except to look after them until they died; there was no effective treatment for cancer, tuberculosis, and many infectious diseases now consigned to history, and no understanding of how to prevent bacterial or viral illnesses. Pain relief for long-term conditions such as arthritis was based on opium, which brought problems of its own. Insulin for diabetes or antibiotics for infections were many years away.

The loss of friends

Back in 1835, when Emilia was looking forward to her seventh birthday, all had been well in the Abbey community. A new family had joined them; Rev. Henry Hart Milman had been appointed as the new Rector of St. Margaret's Church, and with his large family he moved into Ashburnham House. Today, the house is part of Westminster School. Mr. Milman duly moved from

Reading, where he had been vicar of St. Mary's Church (now usually referred to as Reading Minster), along with Mrs Milman and their first five children, William, Louisa, Arthur, Augusta and Archibald, their servants and long-standing nurse, Mrs Amelia Deadman.

For Emilia, there was a new friend; eight-year-old Louisa.

Life at Westminster was not a happy or healthy time for the Milmans. Their younger daughter, Augusta, fell ill first. Over many months, the intelligent and lively little girl grew pale and lethargic, developed a cough, lost her appetite, and became thinner and thinner. Her doctor had seen the same thing so many times before but hesitated before speaking the dreaded word to her heartbroken parents; consumption. Pulmonary tuberculosis is today treated with antibiotics, but for little Augusta there was no cure. Her case was not completely hopeless; her mother and father could hold onto the hope that she would be one of the 50% of tuberculosis sufferers who would battle through and make a slow recovery. But in January 1839, Augusta was just eight years old when she died, with her nurse, Amelia Deadman, in attendance. Mr. Milman wrote of her;

"Little did I forsee ... I should lay to rest in this hallowed place [Westminster Abbey] *a lovely little girl, whose early intelligence gave me the fond hope that she would hereafter take an interest in my pursuits and love my poetry, at least because it was her father's:*

> *My child! My child! Among the great and wise*
> *Thou'st had thy peaceful solemn obsequies.*
> *Seem'st thou misplac'd in that fam'd company?*
> *Heaven's kingdom is made up of such as thee.[90]"*

This was not the end of the family's tragedies. Mr. Milman wrote to a friend in 1841;

"My poor little girl [this would be Louisa]*, now my only girl, is still an invalid. I fear she may be for some time helplessly so, though I hope for the best. We passed the summer at a very pretty watering place in South Wales – Tenby – where she seemed rapidly improving; but the mistimed accident of a bilious attack threw her back completely[91]."*

Emilia's friend Louisa died in 1842 when she was just 15, once again nursed by Amelia Deadman. Her death certificate recorded another Victorian term for tuberculosis; "Decline."

Three years later, her mother gave birth to a baby boy, Charles Louis, and he too was cared for by Amelia Deadman; he was just three years old when he died from scarlatina, now known today to be a *streptococcus* infection, and treatable with antibiotics.

Mr. Milman became Dean of St. Paul's Cathedral in 1849 and moved from Westminster into the cathedral's deanery. No doubt and he and Mary Ann were regular visitors to Westminster, their friends in Dean's Yard, and the memorial to their three children, which is in the north choir aisle of the Abbey.

The death toll in this well-to-do family – three of their six children – was devastating to the parents and to the nurse who had charge of them; but it was not unusual in Victorian London. Today, such a death rate is unknown outside of developing countries.

Victorians have sometimes gained a reputation for sternness within the family, and indifference towards their servants, but the Milmans show us a different picture. One can hardly fail to be moved by Mr. Milman's writing regarding his daughters, brief though these snippets are. We can also discern that they valued their servants, and gained their loyalty in return. Mrs Deadman, who had suffered the loss of three of her charges, and grieved alongside their parents, continued in the family's service. After the children had grown, she became lady's maid to Mrs Milman until her death in 1856. Mrs Deadman was interred at Nunhead Cemetery, Southwark, with the funeral service led by one of the boys she helped to raise; the eldest son of the family, Rev. William Milman[92].

The Fatal Smell in Dean's Yard

Among the more colourful of the Vincents' neighbours was the Buckland family, headed by the Dean of Westminster, William Buckland. He was not just a clergyman; he was a geologist, scientist, lecturer at Christ Church College, Oxford, and a man concerned with the wellbeing of the community around him, rich and poor.

He had the curiosity of a scientist, the practical nature of an engineer, and the drive to get things done; he worked with the Headmaster of Westminster School, Rev. Henry George Liddell, to drive through building works and improvements to facilities at the school, to bring the school up to modern expectations and revive its flagging reputation. Part of the plan of improvements was to tackle the big issue that affected the health and wellbeing of the school, the abbey community and beyond – the state of the drains.

William Buckland was born in Devon and educated at Winchester College, and had an early interest in collecting fossils. He had explored the cliffs of Lyme Regis with Mary Ann Anning and secured an annuity for her[93]. He studied sciences alongside theology, and as well as becoming a priest, he lectured at Oxford in geology and palaeontology. A man with broad scientific interests, he experimented with the use of coprolites (fossilised excrement) as fertiliser[94], and discussed engineering problems with George Stephenson, inventor of the "Rocket" locomotive[95].

Many theologians and scientists of the time were looking to reconcile the account of the creation of the world in the Bible with the new scientific discoveries. Buckland proposed a version of Old Earth Creationism, whereby a gap of indeterminate time must exist in the Biblical account of creation in Genesis chapter 1, allowing time for the geological formation of the earth. One of his works was *Reliquiae Diluvianae,* or *"Observations on the Organic Remains attesting the Action of a Universal Deluge,"* published in 1823, which proposed that evidence of Noah's flood could be found in the geological strata. However, as his studies progressed, he came to reject flood geology, and accepted the work of geologists such as Charles Lyall, which showed that the evidence in question was better explained by the action of glaciers.

Mr. Buckland's wife was Mary, a kindred spirit. She was an illustrator and collected fossils, and became his assistant in a number of experiments, some of which were conducted in the deanery kitchen. Their daughter, Mrs Elizabeth Oke Gordon, describes a time when Dr. Buckland was trying to decipher some footprints discovered in a slab of sandstone, and thought they may have been made by a species of tortoise.

"He therefore called his wife to come down and make some paste, while he went and fetched the tortoise from the garden. On his return he found the kitchen table covered with paste, upon which the tortoise was placed. The delight of this scientific couple may be imagined when they found that the footmarks of the tortoise on the paste were identical with those on the sandstone slab[96]."

One of the illustrious visitors who visited the Bucklands in their Oxford days was the English writer and philosopher John Ruskin.

He remembered Dr. Buckland as a man with

"...humour, common sense, and a benevolently cheerful doctrine of divinity. At his breakfast table I met the leading scientific men of the day, from Herschel downwards... Everyone was at ease and amused at that breakfast table – the menu and service of it usually in themselves interesting. I have always regretted a day of unlucky engagement on which I missed a delicate toast of mice; and remembered, with delight, being waited upon one hot summer morning by two graceful and polite little Carolina lizards, who kept off the flies[97]."

Mice on the menu?

George Cox Bompas, a solicitor, who married the Dean's daughter, Mary Ann Scott Buckland, is more explicit about the delicacies served at the Buckland's table in Oxford and Westminster. He describes a family that might keep any kind of animal as a pet, for experimentation, or for eating. When living at Christ Church, Oxford, the Buckland home was full of various stuffed creatures and fossils, and also many kinds of pets; a pony, a fox, rabbits, guinea pigs and ferrets, hawks and owls, a magpie and jackdaw, dogs, cats, poultry, and a tortoise on whose back the children would stand to try its strength[98].

Frank Buckland, the eldest of the Buckland children, was later to become a surgeon and naturalist. As a teenager, he treated the rats in the cellar as pets, and might bring them into evening parties to show visitors. He also kept snakes and would persuade his sisters to wear them round their necks. Dean Buckland, with Frank's assistance, would often demonstrate the effects of chloroform on various animals in front of dinner guests. Frank's pet eagle, his monkey, Jacko, snakes and a goldfish, slept and woke up again, to their guests' amazement.

"At his father's table at Christchurch, the viands were varied. A horse belonging to his brother-in-law having been shot, Dr. Buckland had the tongue pickled and served up at a large luncheon party, and the guests enjoyed it much, until told what they had eaten. Alligator was a rare delicacy... but puppies were occasionally, and mice frequently eaten. So also at the Deanery, hedgehogs, tortoise, potted ostrich and occasionally rats, frogs, and snails were served up for the delectation of favoured guests. "Party at the Deanery," one guest notes; "tripe for dinner, don't like crocodile for breakfast[99]."

Lord Playfair, asked to contribute to Mrs Gordon's biography of her father, remembered Dean Buckland as;

"The most active-minded man I ever met. To all subjects under his attention, he gave the best efforts of his mind... Whenever he thought he could be useful to humanity, he threw himself into the work with heart and soul[100]."

The man who named *Megolasaurus*, and *Coprolites* had more than a hands-on approach to study; when he started taking an interest in where the Dean's Yard water came from and where it went, people were no doubt amused. What was our dean up to now? He was able to establish that the stream that ran through Hyde Park fed the pump in Dean's Yard, and from there, proceeded across Tothill Fields to a pond known as the King's Scholars' Pond. He was eventually to be blamed for occurrences that were far from amusing.

Alongside the wealthy residents of the cloisters and Dean's Yard, servants, beggars, tradespeople and hawkers also went about their business.

Mary Rohan emerged early each morning from her home in the old stables to go to her work at the Queen Anne's Bounty office just a few steps away. The Queen Anne's Bounty charity had been established to supplement the earnings of clergymen who occupied poorly paying livings and who had no other incomes. Ironically, their financial support was being facilitated by the services of someone even more poorly paid than themselves.

If Mrs Rohan complained, it was in a broad Irish accent, and probably not in the hearing of the gentry of Dean's Yard, many of whom did try to help her. It was hard, being the breadwinner for a disabled husband and four young children; the older children were no doubt sent out to beg, mudlark, run errands or do whatever they could do to bring in some money.

The last thing this family needed was a dose of the fever.

Perhaps Dean William Buckland passed Mrs Rohan on the way to his meetings with the Sanitary Commission, where he was taking a role in the improvements to the city, as well as to the abbey community and Westminster School. His ambition was that all homes should have piped connections to the sewers; but achieving this came at a considerable cost to his own reputation, as we shall see.

In January 1848, work began to improve the drainage and sewage arrangements in Dean's Yard. Parts of the sewage system around Westminster had been placed to service the medieval monastery; some of those ancient sewers were blocked or had collapsed. The system was so old, it was sometimes a mystery as to where water came from and where it was going; at times, the workmen threw down some coloured water and waited to see where it would emerge.[101]

Many of the houses, occupied as they were by nobility, clergy or middle-class professionals, had water closets, some of which emptied into the newer sewers, which had been in place since 1838. Some of the W.C.s, however, worked on the older system; they emptied into cesspools in the cellars, some of which, in turn, drained into an old sewer that had become blocked; in essence, that sewer had become a large cesspool, and had been so for years.

Cesspools had previously been emptied by night soilmen (who were usually women and children) using buckets; this unpleasant and smelly job was generally done at night, with the "nightsoil" transported to the countryside to be spread as manure on the fields.

The sanitary commissioners were intent on finding better ways of dealing with sewage than to scoop it out and carry it elsewhere. There was less demand for human fertiliser since imported guano – bat droppings – was not only cheaper than nightsoil but was also a superior fertiliser. There were health benefits too, though these were not fully appreciated at first. Untreated human waste can carry all sorts of hazards – bacteria, viruses and parasites – which could find their way back into the human food chain through being spread on food crops, or through the activity of flies transferring filth from one place to another.

Dean Buckland's ambition to provide pipe drainage for all began to be realised, with a major upgrade of the sewers that served the abbey community. Main sewers were being improved all around London; old flat-bottomed sewers were being replaced with a new egg-shaped design, small end downwards, which improved the flow at times of low water, and so helped prevent blockages.

The cesspools in Dean's Yard and the Cloisters were to be emptied and filled in, new water closets were to be installed, all of which would empty into a new system of earthenware pipes to take sewage away to the main sewers.

All this was academic to the Rohans, living in the primitive conditions of the old livery stable. Without even their own privy, the Rohans had to empty their chamber pots directly into the drains outside[102].

Under the instructions of Dean Buckland and Mr. William Goodall, Clerk of the Works of the Commissioners of Sewers, a team of workmen, which included the abbey's own labourer, Mr. James Ovans, first set about the task of emptying the cesspools. What had been a laborious and smelly job was improving, thanks to new technology. Instead of bailing out with buckets, the team of men poured in copious amounts of water mixed with Sir William Burnett's disinfectant fluid, based on Chloride of Zinc. This diluted and deodorised the sewage. Then they used a pump to transfer the resulting mixture into the nearest drains; main drains being in Dean's Yard, Little Dean's Yard, Great College Street and Abingdon Street[103].

Mr. Henry Burrows, the abbey's porter, was impressed. The Porter's Lodge in the cloisters did not have water closets. The Lodge cesspool received its contents directly from the chamber pots and slop buckets tipped into the drains by hand. The new modern method of emptying with pumping engine and hose was so much quicker than the nightsoil men, and much less smelly.[104] Mr. Burrows had lost so many of his own family to sickness; his two daughters, Mary and Emma, were the only two children he had left. Mr. Burrows had high hopes that the new system of drainage would bring health improvements to everyone.

The workmen were anxious to keep dangerous odours to a minimum as they worked; every now and then they tested for sewer gas by lowering lighted candles, and when the smell became too much, they used old pieces of cloth, canvas or carpet to put over the gully while the liquids were being discharged.

From time to time there were complaints about the smell, from the delicate noses around Dean's Yard, and from nearby Westminster School, so Mr. Ovans would periodically throw some dry lime over the cesspool contents.[105] As he and his team filled in each cesspool with dry rubbish and earth, water tended to rise to the top. Sometimes it found its own way out and disappeared, as cellars then usually had earth floors. Sometimes, though, when the water did not drain away on its own, they called for a lad with a ladle to bail it out. Once the cesspool was filled in with dry rubbish and soil, the men would trample it down firmly to make a solid bed.

Spring wore on; as each cesspool was drained and filled, work would begin on the next. By April, they reached Rev. Mr. Repton's house in the Little Cloisters. By this time, people were not just complaining about the smell, they were beginning to fall ill.

The workmen replaced the old drainpipes at Mr. Repton's with earthenware pipes, filled in the cesspool and installed two new water closets. Mr. Edward Spice, the bricklayer, observed that the cesspool didn't smell worse than usual;[106] but he did remember advising people at Westminster School to close their windows if they didn't like it. Mr. Richard Carter, Clerk of Works for Westminster Abbey, agreed; he didn't think the smell was any worse than you would expect from cesspools that had been emptied, and were being filled in.

According to Dr. Buckland's biographer, his daughter Mrs Elizabeth Oke Gordon, the problems started when the workmen accidentally broke open a hitherto unknown section of sewer, inadvertently releasing toxic air[107]. But the weather was changing, too; when the work began in January, it had been cold and wet. Suddenly in April, it turned unseasonably warm. There was a bad odour, and there was a change in weather; a double hazard.

Mary Rohan was one of the first to fall ill, and Rev. Mr. Repton asked Dr. C.J.B. Aldis to visit her. Dr. Aldis reported that he found their home very dirty, and that 11-year-old Michael junior was also sick. The family of two parents and four young children had only two beds between them, and Mary was sharing one bed with her son Michael. She was not getting enough sleep, because Michael, in his delirium, was kicking her. Dr. Aldis recommended removing Michael from the bed, but Mary was afraid that if he slept in the other bed, her other children would also become ill. Dr. Aldis became frustrated with the family; they did not follow his directions. He insisted that Michael junior should be in a different bed from his mother, but he returned later to find the boy trying to sleep on a table, with his head hanging down. By this time, 5-year-old Ellen also had the fever and Mary was clearly too ill to care for her children and disabled husband. Dr. Aldis felt that he had no other option than to recommend the Rohans for the workhouse. All four children became ill and subsequently recovered, but Mary died at the workhouse on 18th March[108]. The cause of death was registered as "typhus[109]."

Not long afterwards, Mr. Weare, under-master at Westminster School, made yet another complaint to the Clerk of Works about an extremely foul smell, akin to dead rats, and fell ill on the same day. He called in his physician, Mr. McCann, who prescribed his usual cure for such cases; to eat a mutton chop and drink two or three glasses of wine every day. He had prescribed the same to Rev. George Herbert Repton and this had surely prevented him from being ill. Mr. Repton's son became ill, too, and Mr. McCann advised Mr. Repton to remove his little boy to Regent's Park or Oxford Terrace, where the boy recovered.

Rev. George Herbert Repton's father, Rev. Edward Repton, also lived in the Cloisters, and three of his grandchildren lived in his household. The experience of his household with the mystery fever was much less happy.

During April and May of 1848, several Westminster boys and Mrs Lorina Liddell, the headmaster's wife, fell ill; Mrs Liddell was very ill for ten days "in imminent danger[110]".   It was noted that the 11 boys who were ill all slept at the same end of the dormitory.

At the household of Dr. Christopher Wordsworth, seven or eight of the family became ill[111].

Then, at the Rev. Temple Frere's house, his 23-year-old daughter, Louisa, succumbed, and no doubt felt fortunate that there was a doctor in the house, her brother, Dr. Robert Temple Frere; but it was his sad duty on 2nd May to certify his sister's death. Once again, typhus.

At the home of Mr. James Turle, the abbey organist, five more people took to their beds.   At the deanery, Dr. Buckland himself, and two of his daughters were taken ill. This was particularly amusing to some;

"We were among the first to laugh, the other day, at the expression of the eccentric Dean of Westminster, when speaking of the good effects of some deodorising fluid which he had been trying upon some of the finest specimens of night soil that Dean's Yard afforded, that "the more you stir it the less it stinks;" and we should still continue to laugh at the extraordinary result of his experiments, but that they have been accompanied by circumstances of a very painful nature. Doctor Buckland has been observed for the last 12 months poking the decanal nose into every conceivable nuisance to be found within the liberties of Westminster... a friend tells us, that whilst inhaling the fragrant smell of the May in Hyde Park a short time since, he was surprised to see a burly-looking gentleman, encased in a spenser, examining

closely the drain that runs under the daisies there... his
unfortunate propensity to make himself useful has
resulted in a most dread tragedy. Wishing to achieve a
great triumph in his sanitary war against foul drains, he
opened the other day a very bad specimen in Dean's Yard,
and, having administered a dose of his deodorising fluid,
waited triumphantly the result... The vapour arising
from the new Buckland compound has occasioned a most
malignant fever to breakout in the immediate
neighbourhood of Westminster school, from the effects of
which many persons are now suffering - the Doctor
himself among the number... So violent is the disease,
that the common people have named it the Black
Vomit[112]."

At the home of Rev. Edward Repton, the first casualty was Mr. Repton himself; Mr. McCann attended him, and then was called to a female servant; a few days later, he came to attend one of Mr. Repton's young grandsons, a boy of 13. Mr. McCann prescribed one of the era's great cure-alls – a stay out of town. The boy was quickly followed by his cousin, nine-year-old Edith Ewart. Mr. McCann put her case down to gastric irritation due to the change in weather.

Much more serious was that Edith's mother then fell ill. Mrs Georgiana Ewart was Mr. Repton's eldest child. In 1838 she had married James Kerr Ewart, an administrator and magistrate for the East India Company. They had lived in Cuttack, Bengal (then still part of India) for a time, where their daughter, Edith Cockburn Ewart, was born. But Mr. Ewart had died in 1841, whereupon the young widow had returned to her parents in England with little Edith. When Mrs Ewart fell ill, Mr. McCann prescribed medication for her sore throat and headache, and she seemed to improve for a time. Of course, he also suggested that she spend some time in the country and the Repton family relocated to their country seat at Shoreham, Kent, where Mr. Repton, as well as being a Canon of Westminster Abbey, was Vicar of the Church of St. Peter and St. Paul.

Mrs Ewart felt well enough, at first, not to be confined to the house; but then on the 4th May, Mr. McCann received an urgent request to visit her at Shoreham, where he found her confined to bed with *"a white-coated tongue, aphthous* [ulcerous] *appearance of the mouth and throat, great debility, and scarcely capable of speaking; all the visceral functions deranged, pain in the head, great thirst and dryness of the skin, a small quick pulse, great anxiety of countenance, very restless."*

Mrs Ewart died on 8th May, aged 37. She had suffered an intestinal haemorrhage, and the cause of death was registered as "disease of the liver[113]."

Mr. McCann also attended Mrs Ewart's sister; this would be either Mary Ellis Repton, who was 31 in 1848 or Rose Repton, who was 22. The sister had similar symptoms to Mrs Ewart, but in Mr. McCann's opinion, she recovered because she was of a generally stronger constitution.

Most of the deaths were certified as caused by typhus; a disease that causes fatigue, diarrhoea, a high fever with profuse sweating, shivering, headaches and pains in the limbs. Some patients reported a tender abdomen, others a red rash.

What was peculiar about this outbreak was that it seemed to be confined to a particular line of houses, situated above a particular line of drains in Dean's Yard. Mr. McCann had attended a lady from another house in Little Dean's Yard who had fallen ill on her way to a service at the Abbey; she had passed through the arches near a grating, from which came a bad smell, and she then had started to feel faint.

Mr. McCann felt that the illnesses were more due to recent climactic changes rather than the opening of the drains of two months ago; however, he was cautious. In his opinion, it was difficult to define the period of time that a poison could remain in a susceptible person, and he had also heard that some of the boys who were ill were in the habit of playing over a drain that was connected to a privy of the school; and any untrapped drain could send up a *"noxious effluvia of gases ... which could create fever in delicate constitutions and persons predisposed to malaria[114]."*

Malaria is used here in its literal meaning from old Italian, 'bad air.'

Dean's Yard was a flurry of horses and coachmen as Westminster School was broken up and all the boys were sent home. It was too late for two of the boys; Charles Bonnor, age 15, died in the school sanatorium on 17th May. A memorial in Westminster Abbey's North Cloister reads;

"Sacred to the memory of Charles Cliffe John Bonnor, a Queen's Scholar of St. Peter's College, Westminster. Only son of Major Thomas Bonnor, of Her Majesty's Ceylon Rifle Regiment, and Sarah his wife. Born 26th Novr. 1832, Died 13th May 1848 aged 15 years & 6 months. His afflicted father places here this record of the many talents and virtues which for so early an age were very conspicuously developed.

'But now he is dead can I bring him back again? I shall go to him but he shall not return to me' 2 Samuel XII.23[115]"

Samuel Harrison, also 15, took the sickness home to Goudhurst in Kent and died on the 28th May.

Gentlemen doctors gave their learned opinions at the subsequent enquiry. Mr. Freeman felt that the cause of the fever must have been the deodorising of the drains; anything that stirred up the contents of sewers would be injurious.[116]

Mr. Fincham, on the other hand, did not believe the illnesses in May could have had anything to do with the cleansings of the drains that took place in January and February.[117]

Terminology is sometimes unclear; the doctors at the enquiry spoke of fevers that "run to typhus" and sometimes threw in the term "typhoid", meaning "typhus-like".

It seems clear that Dr. Aldis had more working-class patients than the other learned physicians, and his evidence to the enquiry highlights the selective nature of their observations. While his colleagues saw something ominous in a fever that appeared to be targeting a select few elite people in a small area, Dr. Aldis testified that at the Western dispensary, he saw cases of fever most days. This fever was far from a mystery to him; it was as indiscriminate as any other. It was not just the rich people of Dean's Yard who had suffered; among other cases, he spoke of the family he had had admitted to the workhouse in March, the Rohans. Mary Rohan, who had died on 18th March, was, so far as he was concerned, the first casualty of the Westminster fever, and he knew of at least 40 other cases outside of Dean's Yard[118].

But why the constant reference to odours and the change in weather?

Doctors had believed for centuries that poisons were carried through the air in bad smells - miasmas. While miasma theory is helpful up to a point – people knew that rotting rubbish or sewage constituted a health hazard and should be dealt with – it led the Metropolitan Sanitary Commission enquiry up a blind alley. The obsession with miasma theory explains why every witness was asked if they had smelt anything bad; why the sewers were being treated with chemicals, with an emphasis on deodorising the effluent, and why people worried every time they stepped over a smelly drain.

In the days before germ theory, bacteria observed under microscopes were termed "animalcules," but observers did not know what they were looking at; illness, as they knew, was due to miasma – poisons carried in the air, generated by bad smells or atmospheric conditions.

In the 1840s, doctors were being trained by medics such as John MacRobin, whose only differentiation between different kinds of fever was whether it was synachoid or typhoid. The difference was not of kind, but of degree, synachoid fevers being mild, typhoid fevers being the worst[119]. Mr. MacRobin's standard treatments for fever tended to begin with bleeding or leeching, followed by a glass of wine[120].

The labels of Typhus and Typhoid were subsequently given to two separate conditions. Typhus is the illness caused by a bacterium, *rickettsia prowazekii,* spread by lice or fleas, from person-to-person or from animals such as rats. Typhoid – meaning typhus-like illness – is caused by a different bacterium, *salmonella enterica typhi* and is spread via contact with faeces.

This time, it was probably not the water source that was at fault; unlike the outbreak of cholera the same year, that was famously traced to a water pump in Broad Street, Soho. The water in Dean's Yard came from a clean source, a spring that filtered through gravel from Hyde Park, as Dean Buckland himself had established.

Opening the drains may well have increased exposure to sewage-dwelling bacteria; Dr. Buckland himself believed that the illness coincided with the accidental breaking of a hitherto unknown drain. If this was the case, it was not the odour, but the spreading of faecal bacteria by touch from person to person, by contamination of surfaces, food or water, or through the activity of flies, or some combination of more than one of these.

The houses around Dean's Yard and the Cloisters housed Westminster scholars and clergy who would have been in and out of the school. The people who fell ill were known to each other; they were neighbours and in the same social circles. Anyone, a tradesman, a servant, a visitor, a worker, a schoolboy, even a respectable clergyman or doctor, could have gone from one house to another in April and May 1848 and taken the sickness with them.

If the infection was in fact Typhus, there may be another explanation. Westminster School was known to be infested with rats; boys regularly lost candles, bacon, soap and even a chorister's surplice[121]. Likewise, the cellars of the houses around Dean's Yard were infested with rats. At the Deanery, they even made a feature of it;

As Mrs Gordon related;

"These invisible guests, for none were ever seen, were the horror of the servants; but the Dean, to prevent his children from being frightened, told them stories of the rats' clever doings, and how on one occasion they emptied a small cask of choice apricot wine, which his aunt had made for him in his college days, by dipping their tails into a hole that they had gnawed[122]."

Perhaps out of respect for her brother, Mrs Gordon skips some of the detail of Frank Buckland's long relationship with rats. His brother-in-law, George Cox Bompas, tells us that at Winchester school, rat and mouse hunting was a popular pastime for the boys[123] and as a teenager, Frank became expert at trapping various animals, including rats, for taxidermy[124]. Rats were still present in the Deanery in 1849; Lady Franklin paid a visit, along with the Arctic explorers, Scoresby, Richardson, Maclintock and Inglefield, who took a number of white rats from the Deanery to the polar regions[125]. Rats were still present in 1852, when Frank took a friend, Mr. White Cooper, the Queen's oculist, down to the cellar to see them. He stated;

"I am not particularly partial to those animals; but down we went to a sort of cloister, in which probably a dozen rats were engaged: these Frank took out one by one, and described in a most interesting way the habits and peculiarities of each. Presently a large black rat bolted.

"Look out! He bites!" said Frank, but the black gentleman was speedily secured by a bag being thrown over him[126]."

Ironically, it is possible that the Buckland family was inadvertently responsible for this local outbreak of fever. In the obsession with tracking down the causes of bad smells, no one at the time thought to pin the blame on any kind of "animalcule." Neither did they consider Frank Buckland's favourite animal as a possible route of the infection.

When the memoirs of John Wordsworth, Bishop of Salisbury, were written, the blame for the Westminster fever was firmly laid at Dean William Buckland's door; John, who in 1848 was nearly five years old, was described as *"an active and fairly healthy child, till he suffered like many others from the 'drain fever' as it was called, due to the reckless amateur sanitation of Dean Buckland in opening the immemorial cesspools of the Abbey precincts[127]."*

The memoirs of Rev. H.G. Liddell were a little more cautious, and suggested that the unhealthiness of Westminster was both accidental and temporary, but even in 1899, the fever was still being attributed to the tapping of "a source of malaria[128]."

Mrs Gordon records that the Dean felt "deeply wounded when this outbreak of fever was ascribed to his sanitary reforms... He was far ahead of his day in sanitary science, and, like sanitary reformers of the present time, met with endless objections to his advice to 'clean up'."[129]

One of these objections was expressed in the Weekly Chronicle, a mouthpiece of the MP for Sheffield, Sir Henry George Ward.

"Much as we regret the sad consequences of Dr. Buckland's inconsiderateness we yet think it will prove of great use to the progress of Sanitary Reform. It will put a stop, we trust, for ever, to any attempt to temporise with the evils of improper drainage... deodorising fluids (are) liable to produce the most deadly results when in combination with otherwise harmless nuisances."[130]

The conclusion of the Sanitary Commission, however, was that the cleansing of the cesspools in February, at a time of cold weather, could not have been the cause of fever in May; therefore the main cause must have been the outbreak of warmer weather.[131]

The death of Mrs Vincent at Beulah Spa

21 Dean's Yard, the Chapter Clerk's house, as one of the newer houses, already had the mod. cons. of piped water, and water closets connected with pipes to the

main sewer, but Emilia's home suffered its share of heartbreak that year.

Her mother, Mrs Emilia Elizabeth Vincent, was fading away. She had probably been ill for some time, probably in pain, and suffering water retention, jaundice, sickness and diarrhoea.

It is possible that her illness was caused or exacerbated by the same sickness that afflicted the rest of Dean's Yard that spring, but there is no firm evidence to connect the two; however her cause of death was recorded in a similar way to that of Mrs Georgiana Ewart five months earlier. Her death certificate records that she died from dropsy of the liver; oedema, or swelling, caused by water retention, in turn caused by liver disease. This had been diagnosed within the last two months, meaning that liver disease had probably been progressing unnoticed for some time. Her illness could have been caused by any number of factors; poor quality food or water, intestinal parasites, or a previous attack of a typhus-like illness, like the one suffered in Dean's Yard in the spring. Since most conditions were treated with bleeding, alcohol and laudanum, it was also possible for someone to damage their liver with too much medicine, or through straightforward substance abuse.

When for most ailments, a country or seaside holiday would be recommended, and spa waters were considered especially good for liver complaints, Mrs Vincent was at least of the class that could do such things.

In those days, one didn't have to travel all that far from Westminster to find the countryside. When the Westminster boys went home and the families of Westminster's clergy retreated to their country parsonages, it seems that the Vincents transferred to Upper Norwood, near Croydon, close to the growing spa resort of Beulah Spa.

In 1832, George Hume Weatherhead had described the medicinal saline spring that gushed from a hillside at Beulah, on the estate of J.D. Smith, Esquire, *"embosomed in a wood of oaks... in a space of more than 25 acres[132]."*

There was an elegant rustic lodge at the entrance, gardens laid out by Decimus Burton, terraces, woods and paths with views of beautiful countryside and on a clear day, a view of Windsor Castle.

The growing popularity of spas meant that a holiday resort grew up around Beulah Spa, just as seaside resorts were growing at coastal towns such as Brighton in Sussex, Bournemouth in Dorset, and Clevedon in Somerset. Beulah Spa had all the facilities for a very pleasant day trip or holiday; there was a bandstand and a programme of entertainments, and hotels and boarding houses in the surrounding area.

Dr. Weatherhead's publication exalts the medicinal qualities of the spring; its unique blend of minerals, sodium and magnesium salts were, in his opinion, superior even to the spring at Cheltenham[133], and of medicinal use as an aperient (laxative), diuretic and alterative (tonic). He saw especial value in taking the water for liver complaints. He recommended a pint or two of the sparkling, bitter-tasting water to be taken early in the morning and followed by a walk in the fresh air; coupled with pleasant society and simple food, visitors would soon start to feel the benefit.

It is not known how long Mrs Vincent stayed at Beulah Spa, and if she felt any better for the cleaner air and water of the countryside. The treatment was certainly more benign than others that might be prescribed; her physicians would probably have bled her, either with a sharp instrument or with leeches.

She may have been prescribed remedies such as those recommended by Dr. Edward Seymour in 1837; in addition to copious bleeding, these included rubbing the abdomen with *liniment hydragyri* (which contained mercury, camphor and ammonia), and various combinations of calomel (mercury again), senna, tartaric acid, dandelion, saltpetre (potassium nitrate), quinine with sulphuric acid and cardamom, potassium iodide and elderberry juice. The aim was to reduce the oedema by reducing the amount of fluid generally in the body, by means of purging and micturition. More drastically, her physician may have used a trochar (a sharp instrument still in use today) to puncture the abdomen and allow the fluid to drain away[134]. In the last resort, her pain would have been relieved with opium and alcohol.

We can only hope that the pleasant surroundings and waters of Beulah Spa helped to make the last stage of Mrs Vincent's life more comfortable; she died on 5th September 1848 at a house in Pawsons Road, Norwood, no doubt with her family around her, and her brother, Jenkin Edward Tappenden by her side[135].

Figure 8; Beulah Spa, Norwood. Drawing by A Harrison

Chapter eight: A decade of joy and sadness

Two spinster ladies

In 1851, Emilia Vincent was 22, living with her elder sister Hannah, brother Francis and widowed father, George Giles. Her eldest brother, George, had his own legal practice in Putney, where he lived with his wife Caroline and their four young children.

Francis was still at home and working as a civil servant for H.M. Commissioners of Woods and Forestry at Whitehall Place. Rev. Thomas Vincent was by this time a Church of England curate in Wantage and helping Rev. William John Butler establish the Sisterhood of the Community of St. Mary the Virgin. Her sister Mary Margaret was married and caring for her first baby, Georgina Mary.

At 22, a woman of the working class would have been at work for years. There was no shortage of work for women in the city. For ladies, though, respectable options were few. Emilia's education would have prepared her to be a wife and mother and to run a household; to be an employer of servants, to oversee household finances and entertain guests. A lady who needed to work for money could be a governess, either live-in or daily, or work in one of the small number of private schools for girls. Nursing for ladies was still a controversial option; Florence Nightingale had to overcome considerable family opposition, but in 1851 was writing anonymously about receiving basic training as a nurse at Kaiserworth, Germany.

A lady who did not need to work for money, nevertheless, had choice; the world of voluntary work opened up more opportunities and in Westminster, there was plenty to choose from. There were schools for the poor, Westminster Hospital, which welcomed "lady visitors" close by, the workhouse, or one of the many charities around Dean's Yard that could have occupied Hannah and Emilia's time. Alternatively, they could simply have befriended some of the many poverty-stricken families in the neighbourhood.

The Vincent family no doubt admired the great philanthropists, the likes of George Peabody and Angela Burdett-Coutts, the famous heiress. Miss Burdett-Coutts was fabulously wealthy, and probably the Victorian era's most famous philanthropist. She funded homes for the poor, churches, hospitals, care homes, and was involved with Charles Dickens in opening Urania Cottage, a home for fallen women[136].

Emilia's sisters had set different examples; she could choose the single life, like Hannah, or marriage and children, like Mary. While formal educational opportunities were few, women could pursue study privately; Anna Thynne, or Lady John Thynne, to give her her formal title, was the wife of the sub-dean of Westminster, and in the privileged position of having a substantial staff (11 servants in the census of 1851) to help raise their ten children. She found the time to study marine life and invent a method for establishing a marine aquarium[137].

Another neighbour and wife of the Dean, Mary Buckland, shared her husband's interest in nature and science and was also heavily involved in the social work of Westminster; among her charitable projects was a coffee house in Pye Street, in the heart of the Devil's Acre, which was intended as a meeting place, library and place to attend lectures. Unfortunately, it developed a reputation as a meeting place for the planning of burglaries and it closed. Another project was an industrial school for street boys, and another solicited donations from well-off people, including her own husband, to fund a loan scheme for those in hardship[138].

Social work in the Victorian period was mostly under the auspices of the church; and the Anglican church, in London, was expanding, aiming to meet the needs not just of an expanding population, but specifically the needs of the poor. Along with new churches, such as St. Matthew's in Great Peter Street, Westminster, and St. Gabriel's in Pimlico, there were new missions, with the glaring social conditions of London in their sights; poverty, prostitution, child-labour and over-crowded slums.

The blatantly obvious juxtaposition of the rich and poor in Westminster may well have helped Emilia realise the importance of the family ties that had sheltered and protected members of her own family at times of vulnerability. For many years, she was a dutiful daughter and sister, and attended to caring duties within her own family.

A decade of weddings, baptisms and funerals

In October 1850, the marriage of Mary Margaret Vincent to Charles St. Clare Bedford had been a joyous event in the Abbey community. Rev. Thomas Vincent, brother of the bride, came from Wantage to perform the ceremony at St. Margaret's church and the family gathered to celebrate and give the happy couple their gifts and congratulations.

Mr. Bedford was a solicitor, and the coroner for Westminster, and already a member of the family since his cousin Caroline was Mary's sister-in-law, the wife of George Vincent junior. Not long after the wedding, Mary was whispering to her sisters, perhaps a little embarrassed at this admission to having an intimate married life, that she was *enceinte* - pregnant.

This was an anxious time for the Vincents; childbirth was notoriously dangerous for both child and mother, and there would be few effective interventions if something were to go wrong. In the days before routine check-ups, tests and scans, conditions and abnormalities that would be treatable today went undetected until it was too late.

During the period of Mary's pregnancy, family concerns also centred around George Vincent, the eldest of Emilia's brothers, and his wife Caroline. Caroline had been suffering for six years with consumption (tuberculosis), and George had been ill for five years, with a cerebral condition, possibly following a stroke, and he had become frail. Unable to continue working, George's debts had mounted and the couple had increasingly depended on his father to provide for them and their four young children[139].

It was widely assumed at that time that any single females of the family ought to take on any caring that came to be necessary. It's hard not to imagine Hannah and Emilia dividing their time between the houses, to Putney to visit George and Caroline, and to Dartmouth Street to check on Mary and her advancing pregnancy. George and Caroline faced increasing struggles with their health; as they became less and less able to manage their own affairs, Hannah and Emilia would have instructed their servants, ensured constant supplies of food and fuel, and kept in contact with their physicians.

As ladies, of course, they would have instructed George and Caroline's governess and two servants rather than do any of the work themselves; or if they ever lit a fire, fetched the tea or cleaned something, they would never have admitted it in polite society. There was also a nurse in residence – Mrs Kezia Griffin[140] – who took care of George and Caroline as their physical conditions declined.

George died in March 1851 at the age of 43, from "softening of the brain" (possibly the result of a stroke)[141], with Mrs Griffin in attendance. His wife Caroline died from phthisis (pulmonary tuberculosis), just a year later, at the age of 41[142]. Their four children, Caroline Maria (14), Charles Greaves (13), Sarah Alice (8) and Walter George (7), were left orphans, and their maiden aunts, Hannah and Emilia, thereafter took responsibility for them.

Mary, in the more comfortable situation of having a wealthy husband and good health, looked forward to her sisters' visits, and the family rejoiced to welcome the honeymoon baby, Georgina Mary, who arrived in August 1851.

In 1853, there was a second happy event for Mr. and Mrs Bedford; the birth of their second daughter, Emmeline Elizabeth.

In 1854, there was fresh excitement and a trip to the Isle of Wight, where Emilia's brother Francis married a Worsley cousin, Cecilia Eliza.

Then on 23 April 1855, a third daughter for Charles and Mary Bedford, whom they named Mary Desborough. The three little girls had two doting aunts in Hannah and Emilia, and no doubt saw a lot of their cousins, Caroline, Charles, Sarah and Walter. Another new cousin arrived in October that year, with the birth of Emilia Margaret to Francis and Cecilia.

Meanwhile in Great College Street, Uncle Jenkin and Aunt Jemima were becoming more in need of extra support. The elderly brother and sister went to live with their niece, Mrs Annie Terry, at Dummer, and ended their days in beautiful Hampshire countryside, Aunt Jemima in 1855 and Uncle Jenkin Edward in 1856.

In January 1857, another happy event was expected; Mary Margaret Bedford was expecting again. Childbirth was still risky, but after having been safely delivered of three healthy daughters, surely all would be well with the fourth?

Then disaster struck the family. Piecing it together from official records reveals a sadness rarely seen in the 21st century, but then was all too common.

On 28th January 1857, an announcement appeared in the Births column of the *Morning Chronicle*;

On "25th inst., at 44 Eastbourne Terrace, to the wife of Charles St. Clare Bedford, Esq., a daughter, stillborn."

This was a sad loss after their three healthy girls, but worse was to come. Mary died a little over two weeks later, on 5th February, and the cause was puerperal fever – also known as childbed fever. This may indicate that Mary had needed surgical intervention.

The announcement of a stillbirth in those days could conceal the horror of an obstructed birth; in an attempt to save the mother, a "stuck" baby was sometimes cut out of her and removed in pieces, with no anaesthetic. Every Victorian doctor had the tools in his bag; a terrible preparation for a terrible job to be done.

Knowledge that was still filtering through the medical world at that time was the necessity for good hygiene in medicine, which was practised in some places, but was still controversial and resisted in others.

As early as 1795, Alexander Gordon in Aberdeen had published his theory that puerperal fever was a disease unwittingly transmitted by doctors and nurses, in his *"Treatise on Puerperal Fever."*

Thomas Watson, at King's College Hospital, London, in 1842, had recommended washing with chlorine solution and that medical attendants should change clothes in between patients, to avoid cross infection.

Oliver Wendell Holmes in Massachusetts, in 1843, had recommended washing of hands and changing of clothes between patients.

From 1847, Ignaz Semmelweiss in Vienna had instituted a regime of handwashing with calcium hypochlorite and the number of deaths in sufferers of fever after childbirth had reduced from 20% to 2%.

All these initiatives were ridiculed. There was pride among doctors in working and even operating in blood-stiffened frock coats, the gorier the better. This macho pride came at the expense of the women who died from infection; the death rate had steadily climbed along with the rising numbers of women giving birth in hospital.

The knowledge that simple hygiene saves lives came too late for the 34-year-old Mrs Bedford. She died in pain and fever, having already lost her baby. Her cousin, Rev. William Vincent came from Islington to officiate at her funeral and she was buried at All Souls' Cemetery, Kensal Green.

Meanwhile, Emilia's second eldest brother, Francis William, had been ill for most of his 39th year. He had tuberculosis, and in his case it progressed rapidly, over the course of ten months. During 1857, he went to live in a house near the sea in Cannon Place, Brighton, probably on medical advice. At some point, the news passed through the Vincent family that Francis was seriously ill and not likely to pull through; he died on 8th August, with his brother, Rev. Thomas at his side[143]. He left a young widow, Cecilia Eliza and two-year-old daughter, Emilia Margaret. His cousin, Rev. Stephen Terry conducted the funeral at Kensal Green.

It was thus a reduced and subdued family who travelled to Wantage in October 1857 for the wedding of Rev. Thomas Vincent to Dora Watkins.

Then in 1859, George Giles Vincent, at 84 years old, having buried two wives and four children, simply collapsed in Dean's Yard and died a few hours later.

He left an estate of under £7,000, the majority of which was split six ways; George Giles had six children who survived to adulthood, but three had died before him. The share that would have gone to George, Francis and Mary was divided among their children. His will notes that he had advanced George a considerable sum to set him up in a legal partnership and to pay debts; this was deducted from his inheritance. A codicil had been added, written after he discovered the level of debt left by Francis when he died, and provision was made for this[144].

Chapter nine: Gally Hill, Church Crookham

It's not hard to work out why someone who had lived all her life in Westminster, close to the great and the good, would move away. It's likely that, with all others of their class, the Vincent family would have escaped to the country regularly, and especially in the summer, when the heat would have made the smells and squalor of Westminster unbearable. They were also at the level of income where holidays were affordable, and trips to the country or the seaside, perhaps visiting the relatives who lived in Hampshire or Sussex, would have been pleasurable and beneficial to health.

The few years before, with the successive losses of so many close relatives had been difficult and stressful. The need for a change of air and atmosphere most likely became pressing; in addition, the Vincents would have needed to vacate 21 Dean's Yard for the new Chapter Clerk, Charles St. Clare Bedford.

As a result, in 1861, Emilia was living in a very different place from Westminster; though for how long or short a time is not known.

Church Crookham, Hampshire, in 1861 was a small, quiet village, but accessible by South Western railway trains, from Fleet Pond station. Emilia Vincent was living in a house near Christ Church at Gally Hill, with two nieces, George and Caroline's daughters; 24-year-old Caroline and 19-year-old Sarah; plus her late sister Mary's small daughters; Georgina (9), Emmeline (7) and Mary (5) Bedford.

It's not hard to surmise that Hannah and Emilia would have taken a prominent role in their nieces' lives; it would have been natural for the Vincents in Dean's Yard to take in the young orphans, and for their maiden aunts Hannah and Emilia to take the lead in their upbringing.

At this time, however, it seems that Hannah herself was unwell and in need of peace and quiet. While her young nieces were with Emilia in Church Crookham, Hannah had taken a quiet cottage in Sunninghill, Old Windsor, with just one servant, Esther Elizabeth Rolls, in attendance. The Wells Inn at Sunninghill was famed for its chalybeate (iron-rich) spa, which attracted exclusive, even royal, patrons; perhaps Hannah was also a customer.

Church Crookham was tiny but expanding, thanks to Christ Church, the recently completed Anglo-Catholic church, where Rev. Anthony Cottrell Lefroy was the vicar. The Lefroys were connected with the country gentry of Hampshire, and in the previous generation, with Jane Austen. They were also related to the Terrys, Emilia's relatives through the Bonnetts.

Also living at the house, next to the school in Gally Hill, were two servants; Elizabeth Bristow, retained from Dean's Yard, and Eliza Coombes, who was the little girls' nurse from the Bedford household. Walter George Vincent at this time was away at school in Oxford, but his brother, Charles Greaves Vincent, was living in a lodging near to Gally Hill, perhaps having given up his room for his small cousins to visit.

The Bedford nieces returned to Westminster to live at 21 Dean's Yard, with their father, who had succeeded George Giles Vincent as Chapter Clerk, and his second wife, Harriet Emma Broughton, daughter of a Metropolitan police magistrate. A year later, there was more sad news; the new Mrs Bedford's first child, the only son of the family, was stillborn. Her second child, Emma Julia Vivian, arrived safely in the summer of 1866.

Emilia and Hannah returned to London and lived for a while in an apartment at 8 Dorset Place (later renamed Gloucester Place), until Hannah died from pleuropneumonia in 1865, cared for by her sister. Rev. William Vincent once again officiated at the funeral of a cousin, at All Souls' cemetery, Kensal Green.

In 1868, Caroline Maria Vincent married an army officer, Major Herbert George Bowden, late of the 22nd Regiment of Foot, and they moved to Troqueer, Dumfries, Scotland. Her sister, Sarah Alice, went with her to Scotland, and 10 years later, became the wife of Seymour Montague Leslie and step-mother to the children from his first marriage. Mr. Leslie was the second son of James Edmund Leslie of Leslie Hill, Ballymoney, Ireland, and worked at the Probate Office in London. The new Mr. and Mrs Leslie thereafter lived in Kensington, London.

Only one of the Bedford nieces married; Mary Desborough Bedford became Mrs John Lydekker and moved to Harpenden, Hertfordshire, where memorials to the Lydekker family can be found in St. Nicholas' Church. Georgina, Emmeline and Emma Bedford remained single and lived together for the rest of their lives, at Oxford Terrace, London.

Part two; Emilia alone

Chapter one: Faith and Mission

Emilia's family caring duties came to an end with the death of Hannah and with her young nephews and nieces independent. The question again arose of how she was to spend her life, now that there was no one left to demand her attention. Many ladies in her position would have gone to live with a sibling, and it is entirely possible that Emilia did so, at least for a while; her only surviving brother, Rev. Thomas Vincent was by this time Rector of Pusey, Berkshire, and he and Dora had three children, George, Thomas Augustine and Dorothea.

The Christian faith took a central place in Emilia's life, and there is no doubt that it shaped the decisions she made next.

During her lifetime, there had been significant developments within the Anglican church.

The Anglo-Catholic movement within the Church of England, with figureheads such as John Henry Newman, John Keble and Edward Pusey emphasised the traditional doctrine and sacraments of the church and sought to restore some of the liturgical and sacramental traditions they felt had been lost with the Reformation. They opposed both theological liberalism and the evangelical wing of the day, which had been influenced by John Wesley and Methodism.

Some Anglo-Catholic initiatives, such as the use of candles, clergy vestments, weekly Eucharistic services, and using a mixed chalice of water and wine, were highly controversial to begin with and even led to prosecutions, such as that of Father Mackonochie of St. Albans, Holborn[145]. A constant accusation was that the Anglo-Catholic movement was trying to take the church back to

Rome, and some high-profile conversions to Catholicism seemed to confirm this. John Henry Newman was received into the Roman Catholic church in 1845, and later became a Cardinal of that church.

The Anglo-Catholic movement was both evangelistic and socially aware; Anglo-Catholics were fully convinced that the way to take Jesus to the poor was to come alongside them and try to do something about their poverty.

For example, in St. Albans, Holborn, the work of the church included a Sisterhood; a burial society; guilds and associations for men, boys, women and girls; a Working Men's club; an infant nursery; a choir school; parochial schools, built at a cost of £6000 and educating 500 children; night schools for boys and girls; a soup kitchen; a blanket loan fund; a lying-in charity; a clothing fund; a coal charity; a savings bank and clothing club; a shoe club; provision and food for the destitute, and relief for the sick which amounted to some £500 a year[146].

Emilia and people whom she knew well were at the heart of the Anglo-Catholic movement; for 20 years, her brother Thomas was a curate at Wantage, under Rev. William John Butler, a man whose deep faith and demeanour impressed many.

Butler was described as endlessly patient, and having a *"deep undemonstrative love, bent upon the single-hearted service of God[147]."* Father Mackonochie, the centre of controversy at St. Albans, Holborn, had also been one of Mr. Butler's curates.

The social work for which the Anglo-Catholic movement became renowned could not have happened without a new focus on the ministry of women; and this is where we next find Emilia Vincent.

The 1871 census finds her as a visitor at 94 Gloucester Street, London, a boarding house run by Mr. and Mrs

Hall[148]. At the same address were Cordelia Hart and Anne Avenell, two ladies who were connected with the relatively new St. Gabriel's Church in Warwick Square, Pimlico.

Pimlico at that time had its contrasts of rich and poor; its more impoverished streets were renowned for crime, violence, poverty and prostitution. The area was largely lacking in streetlights, giving opportunity to criminals, and a particularly nasty crime became notorious; garrotting[149]. It was areas such as this that gave the Anglo-Catholic movement the opportunity to demonstrate its social conscience; in Pimlico, St. Gabriel's and St. Barnabas' became centres of mission and social work. Among the priests who served the area was Rev. Charles Lowder, the first Anglican priest to be called "father." He had served for a time at St. Barnabas' Church, before moving to another needy area, St. George's in the East, Shadwell, East London, in 1856.

Miss Cordelia Hart was the third daughter of John Hart, currier (leather processer) of Union Street, Tower Hamlets, and his wife Sarah. Miss Hart became Sister Cordelia in 1871, when she became a deaconess of the Church of England. She would later be appointed as lady superior at the St. Mary's Home for fallen girls in Baker Street, Reading, before taking on a similar role in Hastings, Sussex. There is little to be found about Anne Avenell, but ten years later, she seems to be living in a London household, working as a nurse[150].

It may well be that Emilia Vincent was exploring a relatively new area of ministry for women, that of being a deaconess of the Church of England. The office of deaconess had been instituted in 1861 and hailed as a revival of the Biblical order of deaconesses. The emphasis was on practical service to the parish, and most of the early deaconesses trained as nurses. As the status of nursing rose in the following decades, and the number of trained professional nurses increased, this was later scaled back, but some knowledge of nursing remained essential to the deaconess's role for many years[151]. Their focus was on teaching, nursing and parochial work of all kinds, especially in the challenging areas of inner cities, such as Westminster and Pimlico.

A female of the church could go into households where the vicar could not; they could visit, support and advise the girls, wives and mothers in struggling households. Where a clergy*man's* presence was needed, a mission woman or deaconess could act as chaperone. Deaconesses set up and ran girls' clubs, mothers' meetings, sewing circles, cookery classes, Sunday Schools, night schools and any number of clubs and classes that informed and supported ordinary families[152]. This support was much valued both in the community and in the church, but even so, the role of the Deaconess was very much as a junior partner to the male clergy, as Cecilia Robinson emphasises in her story of the institution of deaconesses.

"The Deaconess is part of the ordered ministry of the Church, owing allegiance to the Bishop and the Clergy under whom she works. Whether she live singly or in community it is as the handmaid of the Church, whose life's aim is to be a 'succourer of many[153].'"

This taste of parish work, in an area of many poor and struggling households, would have been a step well out of the comfort zone of a well-brought up, wealthy lady like Emilia. However, it seems likely that this experience took her into a particularly challenging area of work; that of the rehabilitation of "fallen" women.

Chapter two: Community of the Sisterhood of the Blessed Virgin, Wantage

We back-track a little, to talk about Emilia's closest, and by 1857, only brother, Thomas.

Thomas Vincent was educated at Westminster School, where he was in the same year as Rev. William John Butler, who was later to become Vicar of Wantage and then Bishop of Lincoln. The two friends went to different universities; Butler to Trinity College, Cambridge, and Thomas to St. John's College, Oxford. Thomas then spent twenty years as one of Butler's curates in Wantage, Berkshire.

Wantage in 2022 is a small market town, and thanks to county boundary changes, is now in Oxfordshire. In the 1840s it was generally prosperous, but also had a reputation for its pockets of poverty and crime. The church had generally neglected the town, but all this was to change with the arrival of Rev. William John Butler in 1847.

According to the anonymous writer of *"Butler of Wantage,"*

"Wantage as described in 1847 had a bad name as a well-known refuge for runaway criminals, who found the downs convenient as hiding places from the law; it was for this reason that it was known as "Black Wantage." Serious crimes had been recently committed: there had been a murder at the Packhorse Inn, there was rough bullbaiting at The Camel and, as there were no less than 12 public houses additional to those now in existence and private brewing was common, drunkenness and brawling were widespread. At that time the principal trades of the town were brewing and malting. Men still wore smock frocks and low-crowned beaver hats and women red cloaks with pattens for muddy days[154]."

Mr. Butler's initial vision for the community at Wantage was centred around education, especially the education of girls. He also needed help with the work of visiting the sick poor and other parish work.

The establishment of a sisterhood in the town might be the answer; it would harness the skills and time of an under-utilised resource – the women of the church.

Anglican Sisterhoods had begun to be established from the 1840s, and offered a way for women to serve the church. Sisterhoods represented a considerable resource; the members were recruited mostly from the ranks of the middle and upper classes, because they were able to support themselves. As well as their time, ladies with means also devoted their money and the wealthier sisters made substantial financial contributions to the work of their order. Most Sisterhoods recruited at two levels, based on social class; Choir Sisters were middle- or upper-class, and were expected to contribute financially, and Lay Sisters contributed their labour rather than money[155]. The Community of the Sisterhood of St. Mary the Virgin at Wantage was to be different; there was only one order of sister, a community of equals under their Mother Superior[156].

The Sisterhood of the Community of St. Mary began with the recruiting of Elizabeth Lockhart, who became the first Mother Superior. Two small cottages in Wallingford Street were acquired. A small group of ladies joined, and they adopted a monastic pattern of life, with scheduled worship and work throughout the day. The work initially, was a small girls' school of 24 pupils, with some visiting of the sick.

Sister Lockhart left early on, to join the Roman Catholic Church, causing a double dismay to the community; they not only lost a committed and gifted person, but her substantial income left with her. Her most obvious successor, Harriet Day, was a farmer's daughter, and at first was reluctant to take on the responsibility of leading the order. However, with Mr. Butler's encouragement, she became a much-respected Mother Superior.

The penitentiary at Wantage

The idea of opening a penitentiary, or home for fallen women, at Wantage had been Sister Lockhart's; Butler's initial vision was about education, but he came around to the idea of working with fallen women, and so St. Mary's Home opened in 1849. Rev. Thomas Vincent, already in place in the parish as a curate, was appointed chaplain of the home. Another house was taken, in Newbury Street, and St Mary's Home was formally opened on 2 February 1850, with a capacity of six, later expanded to 30.[157]

Penitentiaries aimed to rescue and reform "fallen" women and girls; they might be prostitutes, or considered very likely to be drawn into that life because of their circumstances. Some establishments catered for delinquent girls; St. James's Home in Kennington was established to rehabilitate female inebriates. By the mid-1870s, the Wantage sisters were managing St. James's Home at Fulham, which catered for those unsuited to laundry work; these were ladies of more gentle birth, or who were delicate, frail or ill. They enjoyed slightly more comfortable living standards, and typically undertook sewing or embroidery work, or some found work as teachers[158].

Urania Cottage in Shepherd's Bush, established by Angela Burdett-Coutts and Charles Dickens, received young women from the streets, released from prison with nowhere to go, and destitute girls who applied for relief.[159]

Many similar establishments were opened under the auspices of the Anglican Church Penitentiary Association. Typically, a girl or young woman would stay for around two years. She would be expected to conform to quite a regimented life of prayer and work, and would be closely supervised. She would learn work skills, and industrial laundry work, in particular, became associated with penitentiaries. The aim, at the end, was that the woman should rejoin society with the skills to find a job, a position in service, or even make a respectable marriage.

Anglican refuges differed from those run by the Roman Catholic church in an important respect; in Roman Catholic homes, the assumption tended to be that such women were irredeemable sinners and would stay in the institution for much longer, even for life. The Anglicans usually assumed that sinners could be saved; they believed that the young women could, if properly trained and rehabilitated, return to respectable society.

Early penitentiaries received hundreds of voluntary applications from the women themselves; other women might be referred by a court of law, or might be offered a penitentiary as an alternative to prison.

Fallen women, in the sexual sense, were victims of the old double standard, for a fallen woman was simply someone who had committed the terrible sin of sexual activity outside of marriage, and broken the further commandment, thou shalt not be found out. Birth control was principally *coitus interruptus*, which was unreliable, but a pregnancy outside of marriage was regarded as the ultimate disgrace in a respectable family. A girl might be disowned by her family at worst, or at best, expected to "disappear" and come back without the baby.

Abortions were illegal and hazardous, and many a young woman hid her illicit pregnancy and gave birth secretly. More enlightened families might do more to support their pregnant daughter; there are many stories of people brought up as the child of their grandparents, and discovering after many years that their sister was in fact their mother.

Heartbreaking stories abound; concealing a birth or miscarriage carried penalties, but hardly an issue of any newspaper was produced without an account of a newborn baby found abandoned; sometimes alive. Tiny bodies were discovered in all sorts of places; in latrines, drains or rubbish heaps, left in parcels in parks and stations, or sometimes hidden somewhere in the house of its frightened mother. Some women turned to "baby farmers" or foundling hospitals with their illegitimate offspring.

At the same time, there were accounts of suicides, as many women, pregnant and deserted, chose to end their lives rather than face life-long disgrace.

Fanny Goss

A notorious case was that of Miss Fanny Goss, a 33-year-old spinster who kept house for her brother, the vicar of Kingsland, Herefordshire. In 1871, the body of a newborn girl was found in the drain from a water closet by the gardener.

The coroner directed that the females of the house should be medically examined, in order to ascertain the identity of the mother. Attention soon fell on Miss Goss, who was said to have been "low-spirited and desponding" recently. Fanny first tried to leave the house and take a train to Barrow-in-Furness, but she was stopped by the police and instructed to return to the house to be examined by the two doctors appointed by the coroner. Once home, she locked herself in her room and stated that she would not come out until her brother returned.

The two doctors waited for a while in the garden, then pleaded with Fanny through the locked door, to cooperate and clear her name. They heard her crying, "Oh, dear, what shall I do?" and started to feel concerned about her safety.

The two men went to look for a ladder to get in through the window; but at length, discovered that there was a way through the rector's bedroom. They found Fanny, who was already dead on her bed; she had cut her arm with her brother's razor and used so much force that the muscles above the elbow were completely severed. They found a large quantity of blood in her bed, and not just from the wounds to her arm. There was no doubt that she was the mother of the dead child. Two servants, a girl and an older widow, who had attended Miss Goss over the last few days, testified before the coroner that they had no suspicion whatever that a child had been born, to the scepticism of the court. The coroner's jury found that Miss Goss had "committed suicide while labouring under temporary insanity." The jury exonerated her brother from any knowledge of her condition, and sympathised with him in his distress[160],[161].

The case caused outrage; we might ask, What about Fanny? What about her pain, distress, abandonment, panic and the sheer terror that made her regard death as preferable to disgrace? Where was the child's father? But at the time, the outrage focused on the attempt to pressurise Fanny into a medical examination. Were women to be forced to incriminate themselves? Men in similar circumstances had no such obligation; just a few months earlier, the case of R. vs Boulton had established that two men, arrested and charged with sodomy (which at the time could result in life imprisonment) had a right to refuse medical examinations that might incriminate them[162].

The female servants who covered for Fanny, even after she was dead, knew very well that the options for a woman like her were bleak; if the father of her child had abandoned her, she faced utter, life-long disgrace.

Figure 9; Kingsland Rectory

Some of those involved in the Penitentiary movement attempted to highlight the double standards that punished women severely for sexual transgressions while the men who were their partners faced few or no consequences.

As Rev. Robert Eden, Bishop of Moray and Ross expressed in a sermon;

"Who are they whose recovery we are seeking? Poor, weak, lost, abandoned women. But who has made them such? Who tempted, betrayed, abandoned them? Who made them outcasts of society? Who ruined and then spurned them? Am I wrong in saying that thousands of these unhappy victims of men's lowest passions have been brought to their wretched and degraded state by men of education, of worldly rank and position, who have used and perverted the power and influence of their rank and station to bring down to misery, despair, and death, the

poor, the weak, and oftentimes the orphan and the friendless[163]?"

Nevertheless, it would be many years before women like Fanny Goss could feel that being single and pregnant was not the end of the world.

As chaplain at St. Mary's Home, Thomas had a heavy workload in addition to the usual parish duties. He led services and Bible classes for the Sisterhood and the inmates, and was involved with counselling and pastoral care.

He seems to have had skills of tact and diplomacy that were often called upon; in the beginning, Archdeacon Manning had some misgivings about opening a penitentiary, and it was Thomas who was sent by Rev. William Butler to win him round.

There had been objections from Mr. and Mrs Burd, the couple who had donated the house that was to be used for the penitentiary work. Thomas was the one sent to negotiate. At the end of the conversation, the Burds approved and wished the work a success. Thomas felt that they had not been properly consulted at an early stage, and that would have avoided all difficulties[164].

He also seems to have performed the more difficult duties of a clergyman with sensitivity. In 1851, Mr. and Mrs Butler's five-year-old daughter, Fanny, died and it was Thomas who supported six-year-old Arthur Butler at the funeral. Mrs Butler's sister, Miss Barnett, described the poignant scene:

"...[Arthur's] one great wish was to be close to Fanny to the last and he had his wish; for when the school children were ranged on each side of the gravel walk, and the choristers in their surplices were ready to carry the little coffin on the bier covered with a white pall, Mr. Vincent

called for Arthur, and he was allowed to walk behind the bier, and as he thought, to help to carry it[165]."

Thomas, in Butler's opinion, "worked like a horse[166]," but his health suffered; in 1852, he wrote a report into the work at the home, and wrote about his own trials;

"Early in the spring of 1852, it pleased God to visit me with a very severe illness; from which, for a long time, it was thought hardly possible that I could recover..." *having spent three months in bed, "it was evident that a full year must elapse before I could hope to be restored to my work.[167]"*

In 1851, Butler had noted in his journal that *"two ladies named Watkins from Badby Hall near Daventry called here this day... They appear quite religious people, likely if they can, to be very useful."* Later, three more Watkins sisters were to *"render outstanding service to the parish[168]."*

One of these Watkins sisters was Dora, who became Mrs Thomas Vincent in 1857, a bright spot in the year in which Thomas had lost both a sister and a brother. One of Dora's sisters, Emma, married James Mackonochie, a barrister, and brother to Thomas' colleague, Rev. Alexander Heriot Mackonochie.

One of Thomas's regular tasks was to produce the work's annual reports. In 1856, he wrote of the many successes of the home; while some of the inmates had not managed to amend their lives, and a small number had died while at St. Mary's, there were several who had moved on into respectable employment or were married.

One former inmate was employed by an invalid lady who had sponsored her place, and another had moved to Australia, working for the household of a colonial bishop[169]. Many of the penitents had been confirmed in the Church of England, 10 in 1852 alone[170].

Figure 10; Rev. Thomas Vincent. Photo by kind permission of the Community of the Sisterhood of St Mary the Virgin, Wantage[171]

In total, Thomas was to spend almost three years off sick[172] and the assessment of Mr. Butler was that he would never be robust[173]. However, he served the church and St. Mary's Home in Wantage until 1868, when he left to take up the post of Rector of Pusey. His friend, Rev. William Butler said of him, *"Our dear friend Vincent preached his farewell sermon after 21 ½ years of fellow-service. May God prosper his goings-out and his comings-in and reward him for all his goodness and efforts for His glory[174]."*

Thomas' long residence in Wantage means that Emilia must surely have visited her brother many times over the years, and imbibed some of the atmosphere of the community; devoted to prayer, education and social work among the poor of the town, and inspired by the leadership of Rev. W.J. Butler.

Perhaps she considered becoming an exterior sister at Wantage, like the Watkins ladies; exterior sisters joined the community for set periods of time, without becoming full-time sisters. They not only helped in the work of the community, they undertook to pray for the work, and to help as they could in their normal life, for instance by helping penitents to find employment or situations. The first of these exterior sisters was Mrs Emma Butler, the vicar's wife, and they also included Charlotte Mary Yonge, the writer who was dubbed "the novelist of the Oxford movement[175]."

In 1894, Miss Yonge wrote to a friend of the early days at Wantage; "...those bright days of progress, when it was such a wonderful home of high spiritual atmosphere and training, mixed with all that was intellectually bright. I enjoyed it so deeply, and shall never forget our joyous expeditions and deeper, more memorable talks.[176]"

Figure 11; The Chapel at the Community of St. Mary the Virgin, Wantage, March 2022. Photo by Kim Tame

Part three; Reading

Chapter one: St. Mary's Home, Reading – fallen women

Emilia did not become either a Deaconess or a Sister, and her reasoning can only be guessed at. The acceptance of women in ministry on an equal footing with men was still many years away; at the same time, the ministry of women as Deaconesses, Sisters, or simply as volunteers, was much valued in their communities. Nursing support in the community was especially valued through difficult periods such as the smallpox and cholera outbreaks of the 19th century[177].

The two orders operated very differently; Deaconesses tended to work alone, one to a parish and were under the oversight of male clergy. Sisterhoods lived in a community, led by their Mother Superior, and worked in cooperation with clergy, but had a degree of independence from male oversight.

A Deaconess was expected to demonstrate a religious commitment; Sisterhoods would sometimes accept applicants who had no particular religious vocation, but who wanted to participate in the order's work[178]. Both offered women a respectable pathway to further education or training, and doing useful work in the community, and not necessarily as an alternative to marriage. Neither order demanded a lifetime's commitment, unlike Roman Catholic convents, and from time to time, women did exercise the option to leave, whether for marriage, to attend to other family needs or for other reasons.

Both of these pathways were available to Emilia; and she chose neither, but did retain close links with both deaconesses and sisters.

At some point in the early 1870s, Emilia moved to Reading, a prosperous Berkshire town, renowned for its four Bs – beer, bricks, biscuits and bulbs. With plenty of industry in the town, and so plenty of jobs, Reading was rapidly expanding and many of its characteristic red-brick buildings are from this time. If you get the chance to walk through the town centre of Reading, look up! and admire some intricate brickwork above the modern shop facades.

Emilia's web of contacts meant that she had several links with the town. Her uncle John Tappenden had been a notable inhabitant, ironmonger and landowner in Reading, but he had died in 1830, when Emilia was only two years old. His grave is in the churchyard at St Mary's, Reading.

A more distant relative, retired Royal Navy Captain Herbert Grey Austen (a nephew of Jane Austen and related by marriage to the Terrys of Dummer) lived in Reading, and later moved to Whitley Lodge. The son of Rev. William John Butler, Arthur Butler, attended Bradfield College, west of Reading.

Emilia's strongest family link to Reading probably comes from the Worsley side; her nephew Charles Greaves Vincent was by this time practising the law with his cousin-once-removed, Jonathan; Jonathan's brother, Rev. John Henry Worsley, had served parishes in Tilehurst, Theale, west Berkshire and Oxfordshire. He would have been aware of the work at Wantage and may well have helped Emilia to make contacts among the politicians and gentry of the county.

Reading was well-connected; thanks to Isambard Kingdom Brunel's Great Western Railway, there was easy access to London and the growing network of branch lines connected Emilia with country friends and relatives; the Bonnetts and Terrys in Hampshire, and her brother Thomas, who was by then Rector of Pusey.

Emilia was one of the first ladies to work at the newly opened penitentiary in Reading, St. Mary's Home at 8 Russell Terrace (which later became part of Baker Street), a building that had previously been a school run by Mr. Farbrother and Mr. Anstis[179]. This was a laundry and industrial home, training and rehabilitating "fallen" and delinquent girls.

St. Mary's Home opened in July 1872 with a service held in the small chapel on the site. Mr. Strickland, the organist from St. Mary's, Reading, played the chapel's harmonium, and a full choir was in attendance.

The Rev. Dr. John MacKarness, Bishop of Oxford, preached a sermon, with a text from Jesus' parable of the prodigal son, recorded in Luke's gospel, a classic text in the story of Christian redemption; that sinners may come home and receive love and forgiveness.

"... My brethren, we say to them that the love of God is ready to welcome them... go and say to them, my sisters, come to a place where you shall find loving hearts, where there shall be examples of living purity and kindness, and hands stretched forward until you have recovered your peace and found perfect pardon... where in honest industry and meek obedience they may pass their days and nights sanctified by prayer and praise and be amongst Christian women[180]."

Within a year of its opening in July 1872, all 30 beds at St. Mary's had been occupied. Of that number, seven of the girls had already left of their own accord or been discharged for bad conduct, six had been restored to their friends or sent to service, four had been transferred to other homes and 13 remained[181].

Local fundraising was essential from the start. In asking for continued support for the work, spokespeople appealed to both men and women; the following extract from a sermon demonstrates at least some awareness of double sexual standards;

"I ask for alms from all: from the pure of both sexes as thank offerings to God, due for their preservation in the ways of a chaste and holy life: especially do I appeal to the pity of the women of the higher ranks, whose hearts should swell at once with the deepest thankfulness for their exemption from so many of those strong temptations beneath which the needy or ill-nurtured women of lower rank so often fall. I ask you by the mercies of your Lord to cast bountifully, with the true heart of pity, into this treasury, whereby your erring sisters may be reclaimed. From the pure I turn to those of the stronger sex who may now themselves be counted among penitents, to that larger number who stained their youth with this very sin, and now, raised up to better things by the undeserved mercies of their Lord, bitterly bewail those wasted years. But where are your acts of restitution? Where your penitential endeavours to lessen that very evil which you once helped to swell, to lessen that class of sinners which you once fostered and encouraged? Large constant alms offered to institutions formed for the reformation of female penitents make the nearest approach to restitution which is within your reach[182]."

Middle- and upper-class women, of course, were exempt from sexual temptation! They often led protected and chaperoned lives, while young men sowed their wild oats, often with lower-class women; servants, prostitutes and naive young women who could be groomed with promises of love and marriage. These young women were the ones vulnerable, later on, to being labelled as "fallen," if these promises were not kept.

St. Mary's Home regularly advertised for laundry work, apparently successfully. By 1881, they had won a contract from Bradfield College, a boys' public-school west of Reading[183].

By 1885, Sister Cordelia Hart, the Deaconess whom Emilia had visited in Pimlico in 1871, was Lady-in-Charge at St. Mary's Home. She placed an advertisement with the heading;

"FRIENDLESS AND FALLEN. Money is urgently required to place a young governess and child in a home for one year. Address Sister Cordelia, St. Mary's Home, Reading, who will answer all enquiries."

On the same page, an advertisement indicates the kind of cad who might have been held responsible for a similar situation;

"KAVANAGH. You should have asked her parents' consent; and even now, if you wish aright, address her father and let her write to her heart-broken mother. On explanation matters may yet be mended."

There is no suggestion that the two advertisements are linked[184].

The usual length of residence in a penitentiary was two years. This was supposed to allow time for the young woman to reflect upon the causes of her disgrace, and to learn the skills that would enable her to rejoin society. Entering a penitentiary was generally voluntary, although some of the young women might have been offered a choice in court between a penitentiary or a prison sentence. The regimented life of a religious penitentiary was not necessarily the soft option, and not all the young women made a success of their new life.

In 1876, Emily Green was charged with absconding from St. Mary's Home, Reading, and taking with her several articles of clothing. On this occasion, she was lucky, as nobody appeared in court to prosecute her. As no evidence was presented against her, she was discharged with a caution[185].

In April 1883, 16-year-old Mary Ann Crabtree had been at St. Mary's for almost two years, and apparently couldn't wait for her time to be up. With a friend, Sarah Howe, she absconded, and the girls made their way to Newbury. They went to a draper's shop belonging to Mr. Godfrey, where Sarah bought a flower to wear in her hat. About 10 minutes after they left the shop, Mr. Godfrey noticed that a very expensive ostrich feather, value 10s 6d, was missing and he went out in search of the girls. When he found them in nearby Northbrook Street, Mary Ann Crabtree was wearing the feather in her hat. Mr. Godfrey took hold of her arm and brought her back to his shop, and Sarah Howe followed. Mary Ann Crabtree admitted to stealing the feather and attempted to apologise. When the case went to court, both girls pleaded guilty and were sentenced to 14 days imprisonment with hard labour.[186]

Chapter two: The nursing home at Jesse Terrace, Reading

Emilia left St. Mary's Home in 1878 to open her own nursing home. The great Florence Nightingale herself had started her career running a rest home for elderly ladies before she embarked on her more dangerous work in Scutari. Like many ladies of private means, Emilia worked without drawing a salary; and she was not alone in this new enterprise.

By this time, Emilia was not the only single female in the family with no obvious obligations; her cousin, Caroline Bonnett, had also lost her parents, Rev. Charles Shrubsole Bonnett and Louisa Joanna Bonnett. Her three siblings had their own families and were not far away in Hampshire; Rev. Stephen Bonnett at Woodmancote and Popham, Annie (Mrs Terry) at Weston Patrick (she died the following year from epilepsy[187]), and Frances (Mrs Balston) at Stoke Charity.

Emilia and Caroline set up together, in a large house of 12 rooms, just around the corner from St. Mary's Home, at 35 Jesse Terrace, Reading, in a building that later became Reading Bridge Club.

Running a residential nursing home was a respectable occupation for two single ladies, and before the days of care standards and inspections, there was little bureaucracy involved. Anyone could open a nursing home and run it in any way they thought fit.

There was also a gap in the market. The wealthy received medical attendance, even surgery, at home. For those who could not afford care at home, there was the Royal Berkshire Hospital, and for the very poor, the infirmary at the new workhouse at Battle Farm, on the Oxford Road.

Figure 12; 35 Jesse Terrace, March 2022. Photo by Kim Tame

A group for which there was poor provision comprised those who needed long-term support, for incurable or terminal conditions, but were short on the funds to pay for it. There was usually little to be done for someone who was dying, or living with a long-term condition, except to care for them until they died; this could involve intensive support for many months or even years. People in this category were often turned away from hospitals because of the cost of their care, and life could become very difficult for families who could neither afford paid care, nor for a family member (usually a female) to forgo paid employment to provide care. Emilia and Caroline received patients with long-term or terminal conditions who could pay some, usually one third, of the cost of their care.

Training for nurses at the time was basic; the nurse's Bible, and the cornerstone of formal training was Florence Nightingale's *Notes on Nursing,* published in 1860.

Although by the 1870s, Miss Nightingale was suffering with her own ill-health, her work in writing, her influence in the design of hospitals and promoting the training of nurses was continuing. *Notes on Nursing* mostly addressed the needs of nursing at home and sold to the general public as well as to nurses in training.

Emilia and Caroline, no doubt, followed its ideas, which represented best practice for the time, though sometimes for the wrong reasons. Their patients' bedsitting rooms would have been well-ventilated, clean and warm, and with a minimum of items that could gather dust, such as excessive ornaments and pictures. Each room at the nursing home had a fireplace; though by the time I worked at Helena House, most of them had been boarded over. Some lovely, tiled fireplaces remained in North House (the former Croydon Lodge).

Florence Nightingale recommended that clothing and bedding should be clean and well-aired; the bedstead would ideally be iron and there should be no valance, to keep the area underneath, where the chamber-pot was kept, as well-aired as the rest of the room.

The chamber-pot itself should have a lid and be emptied and washed after each use; Miss Nightingale was shocked at the common practice, of emptying a chamber-pot only when it was full.

Ideally, but not usually possible, there would be two bedsteads, and the patient would spend 12 hours in each bed in turn. Part of Miss Nightingale's reasoning, of course, was that there were poisons lurking in the emanations from the body, in perspiration and exhalations; miasma.

Her ideas influenced generations of hospital builders, and many older hospitals still retain their large-windowed, airy Nightingale wards.

Some of Miss Nightingale's advice to nurses presents a forerunner of the person-centred care of today – the nurse, as well as being attentive to hygiene, warmth and ventilation, should be well-organised in the sick-room. The patient's room should be kept calm and quiet, and there should be variety; the patient should have visitors, as much occupation as they could manage, have flowers in the room, be allowed the company of the children of the family, and must have a view out of the window. Food should be as much or little as they could manage, and must be palatable to them – and not left beside them for hours[188].

She had particularly scathing words for the annoyances caused by women's fashion items; creaking stays or shoes, or crinolines that might knock over the furniture.

"I wish, too, that people who wear crinoline could see the indecency of their own dress as other people see it. A respectable elderly woman stooping forward, invested in crinoline, exposes quite as much of her own person to the patient lying in the room as any opera dancer does on the stage. But no one will ever tell her this unpleasant truth[189]."

Miss Nightingale glosses over some of the unpleasantries of caring for sick people; care staff today will don their disposable gloves and aprons to assist clients to use the toilet or commode, bath or shower. They will change disposable incontinence pads and bed pads, and have the used ones taken away in yellow clinical waste bags by a licensed contractor. The nurses at Jesse Terrace and later, at Brownlow Road, used soap and water, bare hands, cloth aprons, flannels and towels, and home-stitched pads, and gave the resulting laundry to the servants to deal with – or Emilia may have contracted with the laundresses and inmates of St Mary's Home to do the job for them.

To perform these essential, but unpleasant personal tasks in a way that affords dignity and comfort is truly a gift of love to the person who needs care; but this is not cheap.

In 1881, Emilia and Caroline were supporting three boarders;

Sarah Bryan, a 68-year-old tradesman's widow. Her late husband, William, had been landlord of the Parrot Inn at Chipping Norton[190].

Louise Henriette Diday was a 26-year-old governess from Switzerland and Matilda Smith was a 40-year-old tradesman's widow.

There were five servants in the household; Marion Gun, Eliza Street and Annie Turner, for whom there is no further information. There was Brooker, who was possibly Sarah Brooker, who had worked for the Vincents in Dean's Yard.

Then there was Esther Elizabeth Rolls, who first appeared in our story as a nurse and servant to Hannah Vincent, in a cottage in Sunninghill in 1861; she originally came from Hurley, a pretty country village on the river Thames near Marlow, Buckinghamshire. Having proved her worth with Hannah, the family retained her services; in 1871, she was living with Caroline Bonnett in Herriard, Hampshire. Miss Rolls would go on to serve the family for 30 years; the rest of her life.

There were two visitors to Jesse Terrace at the time of the census in 1881; Rosa de Pothonier, an annuitant, and Louisa Corps, a visitor, described as a housekeeper.

Rosa had previously been a governess, in the employ of the wealthy Roses of Kilravock Castle, Scotland, in 1841 and 1851[191].

Governesses were sometimes in a precarious position; not quite a servant, but not quite equal with the family, a governess was typically a lady of gentle birth who needed to work for a living. Rosa may have been related to the de Pothonier family who operated governess agencies in London and Dublin. By the age of 61, however, she may have been losing her eyesight; in the 1891 census she is described as being blind. There was very little that could be done for common eye complaints such as glaucoma, cataracts or macular degeneration, or even for simple eye infections. It may be that the Roses, or another employer, had been in the position of being able to give her an annuity when she was no longer fit for work. In that, she was lucky; not all employers could continue to support their past employees. If Rosa was visiting Jesse Terrace with a view to looking for her own future support, she chose well; she spent the rest of her life in Emilia's care.

The other visitor, Louisa Corps, was the daughter of James Corps, the renowned organ builder, who had bases in different parts of the country, including Reading, and travelled far and wide to service and repair the organs he had built. Louisa never married, but had a varied career; she had taught in a London school, and had also been a private governess. At the time of the 1881 census, she was a housekeeper. In 1891 she was a lady's companion in Pewsey, Wiltshire, and in 1901, a nurse in Hornsea, Middlesex[192].

It's possible that her visit to Jesse Terrace was to see one of the residents of the house, or she may have been accompanying Rosa de Pothonier on a visit to see if Jesse Terrace was a suitable place to move to. I can find no trace of Miss Corps in the future records of either Emilia or the nursing home; but in 1906, when Emilia wrote her will, she left a life interest in £300 worth of stocks and shares to her. The stocks were to revert to Emilia's niece, Dorothea Vincent, after Louisa's death. This kind of legacy was a common way of providing an annuity for valued servants. This probably indicates that Louisa had been a nurse, servant or housekeeper in the home, or personally worked for Emilia for a substantial amount of time at some point between the snapshots provided by the censuses. Sadly, Miss Corps did not receive her legacy; she died in 1912, the year before Emilia.

Mrs Sarah Bryan was paralysed; perhaps from a stroke, spinal injury, or an illness such as polio. She would have needed intensive support for all aspects of daily living, and her personal care and mobility needs would make her care expensive. However, she was able enough in April 1881 to help a fellow resident, Louise Diday, by witnessing her will. When Emilia and Caroline moved to larger premises in Brownlow Road later in 1881, Mrs Bryan moved with them, and lived there for another 12 years.

Louise Henriette Diday had come from Switzerland at a young age to work in England; in 1871, when she was 16, she was lady's maid to Mrs Muller, the wife of Friedrich Max Muller, professor of Comparative Philology at Oxford University[193].

By the time she came into Emilia's care in June 1879, she was already very ill with tuberculosis; and when she died in June 1881, she was just 26 years old. Nurse E. Swadling, engaged from the Royal Berkshire Hospital, was present at her death [194].

Louise's will offers a small insight into the life of a governess; although not rich – her estate was worth less than £50 – she had some nice possessions to leave to her friends. Her bequests may also indicate that she had happy memories of her previous employments, as she left several items to the ladies and young people of the families;

To the daughters of Mrs Katherine Monro of Grenville Place, Kensington, she left two rings. To Colonel Savile and his children, a gold watch and chain, a fur tippet and muff, a desk, a large Bible and some books. To Florence Scriven, a seal-skin jacket and muff and tippet of black fur. To Louisa Bazett, a knife, fork and spoon in a case. To Louisa's mother, Mary Ann Bazett, the remainder of her clothing and a white fur coverlet. To Mrs Savile and Mrs Bazett, half of her remaining money, for their charitable causes. To Emilia Vincent, the other half of her money[195].

The Bazetts, in 1881, lived in Castle Crescent, Reading, and had nine children between the ages of 6 and 25[196], and perhaps were Mlle. Diday's last employers.

At regular intervals, Emilia sat at her desk, took her blotter, a new sheet of writing paper and opened her inkwell. Not for her the antiquated goose quills her brothers had to use at Westminster School. She needed the efficiency of a modern steel dip-pen; and she needed money.

"HOME FOR PERMANENT INVALIDS

To the editor of the Berkshire Chronicle

Sir, - May I ask through your columns for help to enlarge a nursing work which rather more than two years ago I was allowed, in some measure, to be instrumental in starting, and with the help of a few kind friends have been enabled to carry on in my own house.

It is for those sad, helpless, incurable cases often by the world at large called "uninteresting" and yet for this very reason doubly in need of Christian love and care to brighten their weary days. They have no hope of recovery to cheer them under their sufferings but can only look forward to an increase of pain and weakness so long as their life on earth is prolonged.

The nursing home is intended for respectable women of the middle-classes who have known better days, but ladies left destitute have also been received. Soon after the work was commenced a lady quite homeless and suffering from cancer was nursed for three months and died in the Home. Another (a governess) [Louise Diday] in the last stage of consumption has been in the Home since June, 1879. The other patients are physically in a very helpless state and need constant care and attention.

I had last year to refuse twenty applications for admission, a fact which I think shows the need of such a Home and pleads for its continuance....

I cannot myself afford a large house, nor can I do more than give my own and another lady's [Caroline's] services free of any cost to the work. The patients' payments (£2 10s per month) are far less than the cost of each; most glad, therefore, shall I be if some of your readers who are blessed with health will think of their sisters suffering from both illness and poverty, and by offerings, small or large, according to their means, come forward, not only to support the Nursing Home in its present small proportions, but to enable a larger house to be taken, so that at least twice as many sufferers can be received.

The Home was started privately, and has as yet no committee or long list of officials; but I am sure that the names of the chaplain (the Rev. N.T. Garry), the treasurer (the Rev. A.C. Daymond) and the surgeon (O.C. Maurice, Esq), will afford your readers a sufficient guarantee for the genuineness of the work.

I am, Sir, yours obediently,

EMILIA VINCENT

35 Jesse Terrace, Reading[197]"

The Rev. Nicholas Thomas Garry was, at that time, Rector of St. Mary's, Reading. Rev. Albert Cooke Daymond was headmaster of Timsbury House School in Tilehurst Road, and curate of St. Mary's Chapel in Castle Street. His daughter was the composer Emily Daymond.

Oliver Calley Maurice was qualified both as an apothecary – the forerunner of the General Practitioner – and as a surgeon, and in addition to his private practice, was one of the early surgeons at the Royal Berkshire Hospital, Reading. Mr. Maurice was the medical attendant for Jesse Terrace, and then the Helena Nursing Home for many years. At the same time, he was Reading's Police Surgeon and visiting physician to Reading Gaol, where he was infamously dismissive of Oscar Wilde's symptoms. It had been alleged, and was widely believed, that the great writer died from syphilis. However, it is now thought that his symptoms more likely indicate an ear infection, which was left untreated, affected his brain and led to his death[198].

Chapter three: Brownlow Road, Reading

In November 1880, a classified advertisement was placed in the *Reading Observer*:

MR. FRANK COOKSEY
HAS TO LET

Brownlow Road, Convenient house, with
six bedrooms, good garden, gas and
water. Rent £45[199]

Unfortunately, there is no way of telling which house in Brownlow Road was to let for £45 (that would be per year).

The Downshire Square and surrounding area, which includes Brownlow Road, is now part of Reading's conservation area. In the 1870s, this part of Reading was up and coming; the houses were new, modern, and connected to gas, mains water and the Victorian era's famous brick-built sewers. The homes had bathrooms, water closets and central heating powered by gas boilers; nevertheless, they were mostly built along traditional lines, with a basement for servants, a first floor with large-windowed drawing rooms, second floor bedrooms and third floor attics for children or more servants.

The street was also close to local shops in Brunswick Street and the streets of lower cost housing from which servants and nurses might be recruited. About 15 minutes' walk away was Reading town centre, with the railway station and fashionable shops of all kinds.

The traditional house layout was somewhat impractical for Emilia's purposes; she had grown up in a large house – 21 Dean's Yard had five storeys – but there were so many stairs; water, wood, coal, food and tea-trays might have to be carried from the bottom to the top, and slops, ash, empties and chamber pots down again, several times a day. Water closets on each floor would have relieved a little of that work; but there had to be a way of reducing the lifting and carrying, which only slowed down the servants and nurses and made obstacles for the disabled and ill ladies for whom she wanted to cater; especially when the ladies themselves frequently needed lifting and carrying.

In 1881, Emilia acquired a pair of new semi-detached houses in Brownlow Road, Reading. There were still attics at the top for nurse and servant quarters, but no basement, the kitchen being on the ground floor. There was a large garden at the rear, small gardens at the front, and the houses were near to All Saints' Church.

For Emilia, as a devout Christian, the spiritual atmosphere of the home was important. When she advertised in the local press for staff, she often specified "Church of England," or "churchwoman" as she did in an advertisement in *The Guardian* in January 1890:

WANTED, a LADY-HELP, to assist
in the work of a small Home for
Incurables.
Power to lift essential. State real age,
and if a good needlewoman.
Churchwoman. Address Miss Vincent,
Helena Nursing Home, Brownlow-Road,
Reading[200].

We are left to imagine what kind of situation led to Emilia stipulating that applicants to work in the Nursing Home must state their "real age!"

Old age pensions, enabling people to stay in their own homes in older age, were introduced by the Lloyd-George government of 1908; prior to that, it was a common occurrence for an older woman, desperate to avoid the workhouse, to lie about her age in order to stay at work until her frailty began to betray her.

Thank goodness "power to lift" is not a requirement of care staff in these days of slide sheets, hoists and mobility aids! We will never know how many good nursing staff were lost to those early care homes because of injuries caused by poor lifting techniques.

Being a good needlewoman was essential; in those days before throwaway fashion, clothes and furnishings would be made to last as long as possible and taking care of someone's clothes and bedding would have been part of the service. For those well enough, sewing, knitting and embroidery were a major part of the occupational therapy for the residents.

There was a room at the house set aside as an oratory, for prayer and reflection; in time, this room was to become a fully-fledged Anglican chapel, with an altar, cross and some beautifully embroidered items, sewn by supporters or by the ladies themselves[201].

Church of England services were held there regularly, including services of Holy Communion, presided over by the Chaplain, who was usually one of the clergy team from nearby All Saints' Church. It's not clear from the records on which floor the oratory was in Emilia's day; later, at the time when the building was under the auspices of the Church of England Pensions Board and a home for the Widows of Clergy, the chapel was on the first floor, as marked on plans produced in 1948[202]. This may also have been the position of Emilia's oratory. There is still a cross on the roof at the rear, above where the chapel was.

In the early days in Brownlow Road, Emilia established the custom of celebrating the anniversary of the home each December. There would be church services, at the home and at All Saints' Church, and an annual sale of work, using the large rear garden to set up stalls of various kinds for fundraising. The sewn items, knitting and embroidery produced by the ladies during the year would be on sale, together with stalls of donated items[203].

Figure 13; rear of Helena House in December 2017.
Photo by Kim Tame

In February 1887, Emilia takes up her pen once more;

"HOPELESS, OFFENSIVE AND INCURABLE

I am glad to see from time to time some of the many sad cases of incurable suffering that exist, brought to light in the pages of THE HOSPITAL under the head of "Difficult Cases." I am afraid the old proverb, "out of sight out of mind," has partly been the cause why homes for these poor unseen sufferers have, until lately, taken but a small share among the many institutions existing in our country. I am glad now to hear frequently of fresh Homes for Incurables springing up in various parts of England, yet many more are needed, particularly some for the very bad cases of incurable illness, or, in plain English, the cases that are unpleasant, and very trying to nurse.

In a very small way, an attempt has been made to meet this want in Reading. The Nursing Home, Brownlow Road, was opened in December 1878. Since then, 30 sufferers have been committed to our care. Of these, 12 have died in the home, eight are now with us, and 10 have left. Of those who died, six were cases of cancer, one of lupus. Of those now with us, four are so utterly helpless that they cannot be moved without the help of two, sometimes three people; and another is a sad case of internal ulceration. It will not surprise those who know something of illness to hear that these very helpless, and often dying inmates, are more expensive to nurse than those suffering from acute illness. Often, they cannot even turn in bed, or feed themselves without help, so that much time has to be given them, and a larger staff of attendance is required than for those who can in anyway assist themselves...

Hitherto, two of the three small houses used for the home have been lent to us. It is uncertain how long we

can reckon on this help; we want, therefore, to raise £3000 to purchase the whole property, and place the institution on a more permanent footing. Towards this we have at present only £300. The two houses lent have been thrown into one and fitted with conveniences for nursing; but the third house cannot be so well adapted unless the property is purchased, and the owner is willing to sell when the purchase fund is complete...
Canon Garry is our vicar and chaplain, and O.C. Maurice, Esq, is our Honorary Medical Attendant. The Honorary Treasurer, D.M. Gardner, Esq, Lindeth, Bath Road, Reading, will thankfully receive any donations, or they can be paid to the bankers, Stephens, Blandy and Co., Market Place.*

Emilia Vincent

Lady in Charge

Nursing Home, Reading[204]"

One of the ladies who had died from cancer was 54-year-old farmer's daughter, Eliza Williams. Emilia was present at her death in February 1886[205].

The house next door that Emilia hoped to purchase was Croydon Lodge, the first house in Brownlow Road, which later became known as North House. It was a four-storey house of the traditional design. Emilia had a clear idea of the kind of home she wanted to create; but some further fundraising was required first. In a report of 1887, Emilia states:

"We used this house (which was detached from the other two) for more than two years, with only a temporary connection upstairs. In consequence of the fatigue and inconvenience thus entailed on the nurses, I resolved after the death of three patients in the early part of this year, not to use it again without a proper

connection on each floor. The space between the houses has been added onto the third house, and I trust by the time our ninth anniversary is celebrated [in December 1887], *we shall have a very complete addition to the home ready for use as soon as the additional income for meeting the increased expenditure is promised.*"[206]

The gap between the houses was filled in at Emilia's own expense, with connecting doors on the ground and first floor; the three houses were one.   They remained one establishment for more than 130 years.

Figure 14; Helena House in December 2017, converted into homes. The 'tunnel' was knocked through to allow the creation of a parking area at the rear. The space was once occupied by two bedrooms.
Photo by Kim Tame.

Next door was the national school, All Saints Infants' School, which had opened in 1865 and next door to that, All Saints' Church had been completed in 1874.   Both school and church survive to the present day, and both supported the nursing home into its Helena Home and Helena House days.   Among the Brownlow Road neighbours, Lord and Lady Saye and Sele and their daughters, Mr. and Mrs Blandy and Mr. Tirbutt, the organist at All Saints, and the Yetts family were also among the home's early supporters.

At some point, another lady joined the work; Miss Emily Morris gave her time for free and acted as Emilia's secretary. Miss Morris and her nieces embroidered altar cloths for use in the home's oratory, and these were used for services of Holy Communion for many years[207].

Over the years, Emilia and her team of nurses and servants cared for many ladies with long-term and incurable conditions, and I have included some of their stories, to help to give a picture of the kind of people who would have sought residential care. Details of their lives have been pieced together from public records; mostly censuses, birth and death records, and death announcements from newspapers, with occasionally colourful details drawn from news items in the local press.

The 1891 census is particularly helpful in building up these pen portraits; in 1851, a question had been added to the census, as to whether the person listed was Blind or Deaf-and-Dumb. For the 1871 census, this question was expanded, and asked for four categories of impairment; Deaf-and-Dumb, Blind, Imbecile or Idiot, and Lunatic (it should perhaps be emphasised that Imbecile, Idiot and Lunatic were recognised medical categories at that time, not the terms of abuse that they subsequently became).

In 1891, the question was not changed, but the last census column is a goldmine for the researcher; it gives a description of the impairment of the patient, giving a picture of the kind of patients the nursing home cared for; in 1891, there were cases of paralysis, chronic rheumatism, blindness, chronic jaundice, liver disease, bronchitis, internal weakness and spinal disease.

Where possible, I obtained copies of the ladies' death certificates and wills, which can help to fill out some details of their lives and relationships. Many of the ladies who spent the ends of their lives at Emilia's nursing home cannot be traced; the home itself left no records. But for these few, the sparse details of their lives at least can emphasise that there are aspects of residential care that do not change; these ladies were much-loved individuals, and the support given to their families was as important as the care given to the ladies themselves.

Emilia's Patients

Mrs Margaret Andrews and Miss Annie Andrews

Margaret was the widow of a master builder and brickmaker, Jeremiah Holmes Andrews of Wisbeach, Cambridgeshire, who, in his heyday, had employed 39 men and nine boys[208]. Margaret and Jeremiah had three sons and three daughters. Jeremiah died in 1875 and Margaret moved to Hunstanton, Norfolk, with daughters Mary and Catherine, who were governesses to two eight-year-old boys who lived in as pupils. Another daughter, Annie was also a governess. A poignant detail in the life of this family is that Mrs Andrews and her daughter, Annie, were patients at the nursing home at the same time. Annie was suffering from chronic jaundice and Margaret from "internal weakness." Victorian diagnoses often seem vague by today's standards, and tended to describe the symptoms rather than give a clinical diagnosis. However, Margaret's death certificate, issued in 1895, is more specific about the nature of her condition. She had suffered from "Cystic kidney exhaustion," for seven years. Nurse Lilian Talbot was in attendance at the time of her death[209].

One of Margaret's sons later made a gift of flower vases in her memory to the oratory of the home[210].

From time to time, Emilia rented out rooms to boarders, in order to help defray costs. One of these boarders, in 1891, was Catherine Andrews, no doubt pleased to be near her mother and sister, who both needed much more care than she could provide herself. At some point she moved not far away, to a house in Western Elms Avenue, Reading.

Annie lived at the nursing home for several more years, but by 1911 she had moved to St. John's Hospital, Cowley, Oxford, and died in 1927 at the age of 81. Annie Andrews was not the only one of Emilia's patients who lived for many years in need of residential care, underlining the considerable expense of some of the cases she took on.

Miss Fanny Belcher

James and Fanny Belcher lived at The Fox Inn, Farthinghoe, Northampton, where Mr. Belcher was the licensee and also farmed 51 acres[211]. They had two sons and one daughter, who was named Fanny after her mother. Sadly, their little girl fell ill with a condition that had been known for centuries, but for which there is still no cure; Lupus, or Systemic Lupus Erythematosus (SLE) as it is termed today.

The condition was first described in the middle-ages and named Lupus because of the wolf-like pattern that forms in a red rash on the face. Symptoms can include fatigue, swollen lymph nodes, fever, chest pain and swelling in the joints. Fanny may also have suffered from round lesions on the skin, which is now termed Discoid Lupus, and if so, she may have been subjected to caustic chemical treatment in an attempt to remove the lesions. The treatment worked to remove the lesions, but in itself could cause severe scarring, pain and distress, since the lesions most commonly appear on the face.

After their parents' death, Fanny's brother Charles took over the farm and the license of The Fox Inn, and she continued to live there with him and his wife, Maria[212]. As Fanny's illness progressed, she needed more care than the family was able to give, and moved to the nursing home in Brownlow Road in 1882. She was there just a few months when she died, aged 23, "after a long and painful illness[213]." Emilia herself was present when she died[214].

Fanny's brother and sister-in-law, Charles and Maria, emigrated to New Zealand, where their family grew to include four sons and two daughters; in 1890 they named their first daughter Fanny[215].

Mrs Eliza Slocombe and Miss Eliza Harriette Slocombe

Mrs Eliza Slocombe was the widow of a Reading solicitor, William Slocombe. He was a man of "genial and kindly disposition... in his profession distinguished and respected... and possessed musical attainments not often met with in non-professionals." He was highly intellectual and a consistent advocate of Liberal principles, and an example of a Christian life. He had been Clerk to the County Magistrates, and Clerk to the Commissioners of the Income Tax, and had previously been in partnership with the late Mr. Weedon.[216] The Board of Governors also felt his loss, and paid tribute to "a wise counsellor and a zealous friend.[217]"

Mr. Slocombe had been a member of the Reading Microscopical Society, whose members studied creatures under microscopes and shared scientific articles such as *"Remarks on the Proboscis of the Blowfly," "Development of Infusorial and Animal Life," "Notes on a species of*

Mallomonas" and *"On collecting and mounting
Entomostraca.[218]"*

The Slocombes lived in Zinzan Street with their
unmarried daughter Eliza Harriette, who seems to have
inherited her father's musical ability, as she became a
teacher of music. Mr. Slocombe died suddenly in 1869,
and for several years, Mrs Slocombe and Eliza lived
together. At some point, it became too difficult for Eliza
to care for her mother at home, and she was admitted to
the Nursing Home in Brownlow Road. Miss Slocombe
stayed closely in touch, and regularly helped with the
home's fundraising events such as the annual sale of
work in December. In 1892, Mrs Slocombe died with
bronchitis, with Emilia by her side, certified by Mr.
Oliver Calley Maurice[219].

It was not long before Miss Slocombe also called upon
Emilia Vincent to help her; it's possible that she needed
help to care for her mother because she was already ill
herself. In December 1890, Eliza Harriette had been one
of the helpers at the annual sale of work[220], but not long
after that, she moved into the Nursing Home and died
just two years after her mother. She was suffering from
cancer; scirrhous carcinoma of the breast with secondary
tumours in the brain, again certified by Mr. Oliver Calley
Maurice. Nurse Florence Martin was with her when she
died[221]. Mrs Martin was a widow with two children. She
later became a district nurse[222].

Miss Slocombe left an estate worth £1,282. She
bequeathed her plate and jewellery to a sister in France,
an amount held in stocks and shares to a vicar in
Australia to be used for charitable purposes, and the bulk
of her estate was to be divided between her mother (who
had already died) and her sister. Her clothing was left
for the Helena Nursing Home and the Sisters of the Poor
at Kilburn, London[223]. Miss Slocombe's level of wealth
suggests that she may have been one of Emilia's "private"

patients, and as such she and her mother probably paid the full cost of their care. Other patients typically paid one third of the full cost.

Sarah Frith Swallow

Miss Swallow lived at the Nursing Home for just a few months before her death in 1882 with "paralysis," certified by Mr. O.C. Maurice, FRCS. She had previously owned a school at 4, Bath Road, Reading, where she employed two teachers. At some point before 1861, she moved to Brighton, where she ran a girls' school in Powis Square, one of Brighton's characteristic squares of Georgian houses a short walk from the sea. 11 pupils are listed there at the 1861 census. Miss Swallow had also lived for short times at Bray and Maidenhead, before needing residential care. "Paralysis" could indicate that she had suffered from polio, or had a stroke. She passed away at the age of 75, with Nurse Lloyd by her side[224].

Mrs Charlotte Ann Noyes

Mrs Noyes, born Charlotte Ann Hooper, had lived in Reading all her life. When her husband, George Noyes, died in 1851, leaving her a widow at the age of 45, she moved with her daughter, Eliza to live with her mother, Mrs Rebecca Hooper at 18 Sydney Terrace, Reading. They and another sister, Ellen Hooper, ran a small school, with up to three girls living in. Charlotte is described in the 1851 census as a teacher of music. Another Hooper sister, Eliza, was married to John Philbrick, of the Reading tannery family.

The Philbricks were an influential family in Reading, and contributed to civic and social life, as well as being among Emilia's long-term supporters.

By 1881, Eliza Noyes was supporting her elderly mother at home, as well as teaching music, but at some point Mrs Noyes needed more care, and moved into the Helena Nursing Home. She died at the home on 15th May 1887 at the age of 83.

The Philbrick family continued to support the home; in 1893, Councillor Philbrick was involved with the royal visit to the Helena Nursing Home. In 1897, a Miss Philbrick performed at a concert held to raise funds for the home.

Edith Marion Satchell

William Fletcher Satchell was the son of a Methodist minister, born in Cape Colony, South Africa. He travelled to England to work with his uncle, James Gordon, as an assistant tutor at a school in Islington. After ordination as a Church of England priest, Mr. Satchell became curate at St. Saviour's Church, Liverpool (in Upper Huskisson Street, demolished in 1970), and married Elizabeth Cundell Batt. Together, they raised a large family of mostly sons; of three daughters and 10 sons recorded to them, two daughters and two sons died in infancy, and another son died aged 15. After a time at St. Saviour's in Liverpool, the family moved a few miles south to Seaforth, and later to Shifnal, Shropshire, where Mr. Satchell was headmaster at Shifnal Grammar School for several years.

It's possible that he made the acquaintance of Rev. Thomas Fremeaux Boddington, rector of the neighbouring village of Badger. If so, they may well have discussed the social problems in their villages. Mr. Satchell was instrumental in opening a working-men's club in Shifnal. He was well-known to be teetotal himself, but one of the aims of the club was to encourage moderate, rather than excessive consumption of alcohol[225]. Mr. Boddington may have been ambivalent on the subject of alcohol, as he was related to the famous brewery family; his brother Reginald Brooke Boddington was married to Emilia Vincent's cousin once removed, Frances Ann Vincent.

By 1881, Mr. Satchell and family had lived for a time in Macclesfield, Cheshire, but were now living in Islington, where Mr. Satchell took up the post of chaplain at Bromley College. At that point, they had nine children living. While in Islington, Mrs Satchell gave birth one more time; but Frederick Batt Satchell died shortly after birth.

At least two of their surviving children gave them particular concern. Edith Marion, probably had some kind of learning disability. We have two hints as to the nature of Edith's problems; the 1991 census describes her as suffering from spinal disease; in 1901, she is described as feeble-minded[226]; if this means she had a combination of physical and learning disabilities, it might indicate some form of cerebral palsy caused by a difficult birth, or a condition such as spina bifida.

The Satchell's second son, Henry Martyn, seems to have been in trouble from an early age. Even more sadly, he seems to have targeted his friends, and the friends of his friends. He was well-educated; in 1879, he left Brighton College[227], and afterwards variously appears in records as a tutor, teacher or clerk – and serial conman.

In November 1880, Henry was just 20 years old, when he went to visit a friend, Roland Benjamin Cliff at Blackburn, Lancashire. Roland was a 19-year-old solicitor's clerk, and lived with his widowed mother. When Henry left, it was with a suitcase, clothing and books, valued at around £15, that he took to Macclesfield and pawned. At his trial, his defence lawyer claimed Henry was in embarrassed circumstances, and fully intended to return the items he took; but the jury apparently saw through the smartly dressed, well-spoken young man. He was found guilty and sentenced to six months with hard labour at H.M.P. Preston[228].

Some of his later scams were a little more subtle, and are replayed nowadays via email.

In 1882, a football team from London went to Borden, Sussex, to play a match at the school. Rev. William Henry Bond, one of the masters at the Borden school, met the captain of the visiting team, and in the course of conversation, discovered that he knew an old friend, Rev. Mr. Belcher at Brighton College. The visiting team left, and Mr. Bond thought no more about it. A few months later, Mr. Bond received a telegram, apparently from his friend, Mr. Belcher. The telegram asked for an emergency loan of £5 and requested that he send a cheque to an address in Barnsbury immediately. Mr. Bond sent the cheque as requested; but then doubts arose in his mind. He sent a telegram to Mr. Belcher to ask if the request were genuine. Mr. Belcher's swift telegram in response, denying any knowledge of a request for a loan, resulted in Mr. Bond going to the police. The police watched the address in Barnsbury and as soon as Henry Martyn Satchell arrived to collect the letter, he was arrested. Mr. Bond later identified him as the football team captain he had met the year before.

Police Inspector McFadden then discovered that there were other cases pending against Henry Satchell. He made a "rambling defence" at his trial, but bail was denied, and he was remanded in custody[229].

In June 1884, Henry headed south. It was Royal Ascot week. He met up with an old friend, only described in the news report as "a much-respected gentleman of the town" in Windsor, and the friend invited him home. Henry then went to Windsor High Street, to Mr. C.W. Seymour's establishment, and asked for a gold watch, worth £22, to be sent to his highly respectable friend on approval. Mr. Seymour obligingly had the parcel delivered; but it was Henry, not his respectable friend, who received it at the door, then left in a hurry.

Figure 15; The Brighton College football team in 1878. Henry Martyn Satchell is first from left, back row.
Photo by kind permission from the Brighton College Archive.

The police offered a £2 reward for information leading to his capture; apparently unsuccessfully, because his next trial was for obtaining a silver watch by false pretences from Thomas Bullock, watchmaker of Chippenham. On the same visit to Chippenham, he left the George Hotel without paying for his bed and dinner, and had given two false names. He was caught when he returned to Chippenham station for some left luggage. This time his sentence was 12 months with hard labour; followed by another 18 months, because the police had by then caught up with him regarding the gold watch stolen in Windsor.

By 1886, Henry was back in court, and his offences sound familiar; in Weston-super-Mare this time, he had obtained a bag and two umbrellas by deception, by claiming that a well-known local gentleman had asked for them to be sent on approval.

In spite of the way he seems to have treated his acquaintances, there was still someone to speak up for him, and the newspaper report of this case contains the nearest we can get to a motive;

"...a gentleman stepped into the witness box and said the prisoner was the son of a clergyman and was sufficiently well-educated to act as a tutor. While so acting he formed an attachment which was not approved by his friends, which was broken off, he believed. From that time the prisoner seemed to have been entirely unhinged.[230]*"*

Henry's parents, Rev. and Mrs Satchell, had moved to Reading in the 1880s, to 19, Addington Road. They were not far from Mrs Satchell's parents, Edmund and Elizabeth Batt, who lived in Eastern Avenue, near Cemetery Junction, Reading.

Mr Satchell died in 1887, at the age of 54, and Mrs Satchell was not far behind him. Sadly, she pre-deceased her parents; she died at the age of 50, when the last of her surviving children, Thomas Christopher, was only eight years old.

Edith Marion, who had been dependent upon her parents, was left on her own; sadly, it is still often the case that when someone with a learning disability loses their parents, they also lose their home. As to her eight brothers, they had by this time either left the country or were too young to support her; one brother was shortly to move to France, three were in Australia. The three youngest sons were still boys at school, and her grandparents were elderly. Henry, it seems, would not have been able to support her even if he wanted to. The next mention of Edith in official records, then, is that she is living at the Helena Nursing Home.

There is evidence that was not forgotten by her distant brothers. Her younger brother, William Edward Gould Satchell, who had emigrated to Australia, named his second daughter Edith Marion in 1888[231].

Henry's escapades were not finished yet; in 1892 he served 14 days with hard labour following a theft of clothing and leaving his lodgings without paying[232].

At various times there were letters to *The Times* and *The Guardian*, warning the ex-students of Lancing College, Brighton College or Shifnal Grammar School, where his father had been headmaster, or any clergymen, that they might be targeted with a hard-luck story.

This letter, to *The Guardian* in March 1899 gives some poignant detail:

"Sir - May I warn your readers against a man called Henry Martyn Satchell, who uses my name as a reference, and for particulars about whom I have had letters from clergymen at Liverpool, Ormskirk, Bradford and elsewhere?

It is true that he was at this school for a short time, but it was previous to my coming here, and I have never seen him. My first acquaintance with his dealings was from his writing a forged letter in the name of one of my former colleagues asking for a loan of money. My answer with money enclosed came into the hands of his mother (Satchell himself having meanwhile gone to the temporary retirement of a house of correction), and she returned it with a heartbroken request that no proceedings should be taken against her son.

As Mrs Satchell is now dead, and the son is again prosecuting his trade of getting money under false

*pretences, which he has followed for 23 years, I think it
right to send this warning.*

DARWIN WILMOT.
The Grammar School, Macclesfield
February 13, 1899[233]"

Henry disappears from public records at the end of the century; meanwhile, his disabled sister Edith lived at the Helena Nursing Home for more than 20 years. The 1939 register lists her as boarding with a Mr. and Mrs Ostridge in Body Road, Reading. In 1945, she was living at 74 Crescent Road, Reading, with spinsters Florence and Edith Farr[234], then moved again to Firwood Road, Camberley, apparently living with a former supporter of the Helena Home, Miss Antoniette Tupman[235]. Miss Tupman had donated her own handiwork, an embroidered altar cloth, which was in use during services of Holy Communion at Helena House for many years[236].

Edith died the same year at Ingleside Nursing Home, Yateley. Her death certificate records three contributing factors; cerebral arteriosclerosis, arteriosclerosis, and influenza.

Most poignantly, she is described as a "spinster of independent means, daughter of – [blank] Satchell, occupation unknown[237]".

Edith may not have had much mental capacity or ability to communicate to start with; at the age of 84, it may be that she was totally dependent, frail and unable to communicate. Once in institutional care, she would have depended on good staff and good record keeping for the continuance of the knowledge of who she was; knowledge that in her case, was lost. Her final carers did not know her father's name and occupation, the all-important details that then defined a daughter's identity and place in society. Given the right kind of support and care, this is not necessarily an unhappy situation; one can only hope that her final carers were kind and made her last few years comfortable.

The fact that Edith lived for more than five decades in institutional care again underlines the enormous commitment Emilia and her successors had towards those needing such support.

Nurses and servants

Nurses and servants proved more difficult to trace than patients; they were a more transient population, and more likely than patients to marry and change their names. Patients once admitted into residential care tended to stay there until they died, making their records easier to find.

However, it did not feel right not to mention the team of ladies who worked at the Helena Nursing Home, even if there is little information about them. They tended the ladies with kindness and patience in a world where nurses were still fighting for recognition as professionals and there were few concessions for the less able-bodied. Their status was still under development, but the backgrounds of Emilia's nurses do show that women with a reasonable level of education and respectability were choosing nursing as a profession. Those nurses not mentioned elsewhere in this book include:

Mrs Sarah Brash, a widow from Scotland[238].

Fanny Cozens, daughter of a farmer and currier (processor of leather) from Walsall, Shropshire[239].

Mabel and Margaret A'Bear, daughters of a gentleman farmer of Rocky Lane Farm, Bix, Oxfordshire[240].

Frances Cox, an attorney's daughter. She was still working, at the age of 71, as a housekeeper[241].

Frances Major, who had previously assisted her parents in running the Royal Exchange Inn in Denmark Street, Wokingham[242].

One nurse deserves particular attention; Miss Harriet Kate Geary was from the village of Beenham in West Berkshire, where her father worked as a brewer's clerk. She spent many years as a teacher and private governess, and then appears in the census at the Helena Nursing Home in 1891 as head nurse. In 1901 she is listed as a visitor elsewhere, and there is no way of telling if her visit was for one night or long-term; whether she was still in Emilia's employ, or working somewhere else. However, she was a significant person in Emilia's life; Harriet reappears in later records when Emilia herself was in need of care, and also as a beneficiary of Emilia's will, where she is bequeathed £100 and described as a "faithful friend[243]." It doesn't appear too far-fetched, then, to suggest that she had spent many years in Emilia's employ, and had become, like Miss Rolls, much more than a servant; she was a trusted friend.

The servants proved even more difficult to trace; there were probably a great many of them, into the workforce at a young age and out again when they married, but only those who are named in a census can be currently known. Following people up is also complicated by variants in the spelling of names, inaccuracies in places of birth, and the commonality of some names.

Sarah Brooker, who was cook at Jesse Terrace in 1881, might tentatively be identified as a servant from Dean's Yard days; she is the right age. As noted elsewhere, Emilia may have had difficulties with a cook who did not disclose her real age; the cook working for her in 1891 was Anne Butcher, a blacksmith's daughter from Bampton, Oxfordshire. She was 31 at the time of the census and so was probably not the one who lied about her age.

Eliza Holdup, 21-year-old housemaid from Newbury, present at the Helena Home in 1891, might be the Eliza Holdup who married three years later. Of Mary Siterms, and Edith Shire, I could find no further information.

The never-ending work of cleaning, food preparation, fetching, running errands and more cleaning underpinned the running of the house and supported the nursing work, and perhaps this is a good place to pay tribute to the (mostly) women who continue to do that work in hospitals and care homes, at low rates of pay, with low status and largely unknown.

Chapter four: Lucy May Owindia

Figure 16; Lucy May Owindia[244]

I was sitting in the Berkshire Records Office, late in a long day, with one more record to look at. It promised to be a fairly dull read. I had in front of me a large red accounts book, containing a record of the Church of England services held at Helena House during its time as a residence for the widows of clergymen, owned by the Church of England Pensions Board. I almost passed it by; then decided that as I'd asked the nice archivist to find it for me, I ought to read it.

Sure enough, it was a fairly dull list. For many years, every Wednesday at 8.30am, there had been an Anglican Eucharistic service held by a vicar of All Saints' Church in the chapel at the home. But in the back of the book, there was a discovery that made my whole day at the B.R.O. worthwhile.

There was a piece of paper stuck into the back of the book, and a story, handwritten in fading blue ink; the true story of Lucy May Owindia, a native Canadian child. Some of the details on the piece of paper turned out to be incorrect, so I have reconstructed her story from the writings of the English missionary who adopted her, Mrs Charlotte Selina Bompas.

Charlotte Selina Cox had married her cousin, Rev. Dr. William Carpenter Bompas, who was the Bishop of Selkirk and missionary to the native Canadians, widely referred to at the time as Red Indians. On one of his brief trips home, he had proposed marriage, and after the wedding, they travelled back to Canada together.

Their connection with Emilia went back to Dean's Yard days; Mr. Bompas' brother, George Cox Bompas was married to Mary Ann Scott Buckland, a daughter of Dr. William Buckland, Dean of Westminster. The Coxes, Bompases, Bucklands and Vincents had been part of the same social networks for many years. Mrs Bompas' sister, Miss Emma Sophia Cox, was a beneficiary of Emilia's will, written in 1906[245].

Mrs Bompas tells the story (please forgive the way she expresses herself at times; it was a different time);

"Michell the hunter was but an average type of the Indian character; of a fiery, ardent nature, and unschooled affections, he never forgot a wrong done him in early youth by a white man. His sweetheart was taken from him, cruelly, heartlessly, mercilessly, during his absence, without note or sign or warning, while he was working with all energy to make a home for the little black-eyed maiden, who had promised to be his bride. If Michell could but once have seen the betrayer to have

*given vent to his feelings of scorn, rage, and indignation!
To have asked him, as he longed to ask him, if this was
his Christian faith, his boasted white man's creed! To
have asked if in those thousand miles he had traversed to
reach the red man's home, there were no girls suited to
his mind, save only the one betrothed to Indian Michell!
He would have asked, too, if it were not enough to invade
his country, build houses, plant his barley and potatoes,
and lay claim to his moose deer and bear, his furs and
peltries, but he must needs touch, with profane hands,
his home treasures, and meddle with that which "even an
Indian" holds sacred? It might, perchance, have been
better for Michell if he could have spoken out and
unburdened himself of his deep sense of wrong and
injury, which from henceforth lay like a hot iron in his
heart...."*

At length, Michell recovered from his broken heart
and married a woman named Accomba, and they started
their own family. For a while, they were part of a native
settlement in the neighbourhood of Fort Simpson.
However, Michell had not lost his intense mistrust of the
white settlers. Mrs Bompas continues,

*"In the middle of the night, Michell roused his wife
and little ones, declaring that the white man was coming
to do them some mischief. Bearing his canoe upon his
head he soon launched it off, and in his mad haste to be
away he even left a number of his chattels behind."*

Michell and his wife reappeared at Fort Simpson one
more time, in the winter of 1880, and with them their
latest baby, a tiny girl of a few months old, carried in a
moss bag on her mother's back.

*"A blessed institution is that of the moss bag to the
Indian infant; and scarcely less so to the mother
herself.... Through a good part of the long winter nights,
the mother worked at the fine beadwork which must
adorn the whole front of the moss bag. By a strange*

intuitive skill she has traced the flowers and leaves and delicate little tendrils, the whole presenting a marvellously artistic appearance, both in form and in well-combined colours. Then must the moss be fetched to completely line the bag, and to form both bed and wrapping for the little one. For miles into the woods will the Indian women hie to pick the soft moss which is only to be met within certain localities. They will hang it out on bush and shrub to dry for weeks before it is wanted, and then trudge back again to bring it home, in cloths or blankets swung from their often already burdened shoulders. Then comes the picking and cleaning process, and thawing the now frozen moss before their campfires. Every leaf and twig must be removed, for nothing may hurt the little baby limbs. And now all is prepared; the sweet downy substance is spread out as pillow for the baby head and both couch and covering for the rest of the body. Then the bag is laced up tight, making its small tenant as warm and cosy as possible; only the little face appears - the bonnie, saucy Indian baby face, singularly fair for the first few months of life, with the black beadlike eyes, and soft silken hair, thick even in babyhood[246]."

Accomba, Michell's wife, sometimes complained about his moods and violence, and one day, knowing that Michell had one of his "ugly fits" upon him, the community stayed away from him and his lodge. Later on, a shot was heard, and the community realised with horror that Michell had shot his wife. Some of the men seized him and tied him to a tree. One of them took his gun and threw it in the river. Some of the shocked and crying women proceeded to prepare Accomba for burial; they wrapped Accomba in her blanket, with her shawl and handkerchief, her beaded leggings and moccasins. She was buried the same day.

Still in shock, the community prepared to leave their campsite since that land was now desecrated. Every tent and lodge was taken down, bundles were packed, canoes were lifted into the water and less than two hours later, the men, women and children were in their canoes on their way to the opposite bank of the river. Michell and Accomba's children had not been forgotten;

"As soon as the first shock of the discovery was over, and the women had a little expended their feelings and emotions in the tears and wail of sorrow, they began to turn their attention to the motherless little ones. First they gave them food, which would be an Indian's preliminary step under every emergency; then, they folded kind motherly arms around them, and imprinted warm kisses on the terror stricken faces; and by all such fond endearments they strove to make them forget their sorrow; for an Indian, passive and undemonstrative as he may be under ordinary circumstances, is full of love and tenderest offices of pity when real occasion calls them forth. It was thus, then, that the children were taken and dispersed among the various families in the rapid flight from their recent camping grounds. The canoes had started, and were being paddled at full speed across the river, when suddenly, to the dismay and amazement of everyone, the figure of Michell was seen standing by the river brink!... The language used by the miserable man on the present occasion was bitter and abusive; it related to his children, who he said were being taken away that they might be delivered to the white man; but his words fell widely upon the ears of the Indians, who only shuddered as they gazed upon his dark visage now distorted with passion; and his whole figure, to which portions of the cords which had bound him were still clinging, presenting the appearance of a man possessed, the veritable Nakani – wild man of the woods – in whom the Indians believe, and whom they so greatly dread.

It was not until the Indians had reached the other side of the river, which at that part was maybe a mile and a quarter wide, that they collected together and became aware that one of the children was missing! That this should be so, and that in their terror and haste to depart they had forgotten or overlooked the baby, still a nursling, who must have been crawling about outside the camp during the fatal tragedy of that morning, may seem strange. More strange still, but not one of that party should have thought of going back to seek her. The female infant occupies an insignificant place among those uncivilised people: the birth of one of them is greeted with but a small fraction of the honours with which a male child would be welcomed.

And into the causes of the death of not a few of these girl babies it would perhaps be painful to inquire; but many a poor Indian mother will delude herself into the belief that she has done a merciful act when the little infant of a few hours' life is buried deep under the snow, the mother's sin undiscovered, and "my baby saved from starvation."

And so the poor Indians of our story troubled themselves but little about the missing babe, and there was certainly a bare possibility 'that the father might come upon it and succour it - for Michell had always been a kind father, that he might possibly find and carry the child to one of the camps not far distant....²⁴⁷"

Meanwhile, a small birch bark canoe was travelling up the river from Fort Little Rapids, bound for Fort Simpson, a journey of about 500 miles. There were three men in the canoe; a Cree, or Swampy Indian, in the service of the Hudson's Bay company, and two Slavès, or Etchà-Ottiné of Mackenzie River. They heard a sound which caused the three men to stop their paddling and listen... a dog? A child? One of the men went to investigate and up the bank, he saw four dogs who seemed to be guarding something. The dogs had formed a circle around a little bundle of rags, wrapping the now nearly lifeless form of a 13-month-old girl. The men cut some wood, made a fire, and gave the tiny girl some tea. Later that evening, they reached Fort Simpson, and found that the news of Michell's crime was already known. But who would look after the child?

Caring for a motherless baby was not straightforward in a time and place where substitute milk was not available, and where fish or rabbit soup would be the only alternative. At first, Minneha, Accomba's cousin, said she would take the child, but found the task too much for her, and the girl was not thriving. One day, a little bundle was brought to the English Mission House at Fort Simpson, by Sinclia, Minneha's daughter. It was Accomba's baby, tiny and fragile. She had been named "Owindia," which means "weeping one." The message from Minneha was, "I am sick. I cannot work for the child. You take her."

And so Owindia, whose father so dreaded his children ending up with the white men, was taken in by the Bishop and Mrs Bompas.

They took her to St. David's Church at Fort Simpson, where she was baptised Lucy May Owindia – May for the month that she was found, and Owindia to keep the name her tribe had given her.

"A visitor at our Mission House at Fort Simpson would be likely to see in the early morning, a small round-faced, black-eyed damsel toddling about, chirping and crowing over a piece of dried fish which she holds in her hand, and devours with intense enjoyment, or if at Prayer time she will be seated on my knee or standing at my chair, behaving with perfect quietness and decorum. In the evening she may be seen crouching among the flowers which have been raised for the first time this year at Fort Simpson; bright poppies and china asters, portulaccas and sweet peas... she loves to look at them, and her eyes sparkle with delight at their bright colours and sweet fragrance. A great delight she is to us growing

in sweetness and intelligence every day... The Indian wives are very good in helping me in various ways concerning her. One woman will come and wash all her clothes, another will make me some of her tiny moccasins, another will paddle off across the river in her canoe to fetch me bags full of the sweet soft moss, which is so indispensable to an Indian baby. There seems to be quite a new link established between myself and the Indian mothers in little Owindia, our last Mission child[248]."

Michell came back to Fort Simpson sometime later, and an attempt was made to put him on trial for murder; but no Indian would testify against him and he had to be released[249].

The Bompases decided to give Lucy an English education, and Mrs Bompas took her to Ditchingham, Norfolk, and enrolled her at the school run by the sisterhood of All Hallows, before returning to Canada. Lucy became ill, and the assessment was that the climate did not suit her; she went to live with Mrs Bompas' sister, Miss Emma Sophia Cox, in Salisbury for a further year. Miss Cox then felt that Lucy needed more professional help, and thought of her old friend, Emilia Vincent[250].

Thus it happened, that Emilia, by now experienced in nursing and supporting elderly ladies, was suddenly presented with a very sick little girl.

We can only imagine the sinking feeling in Emilia's heart as she takes charge of Lucy and notes the wasting, the coughing and the weakness; and the stirring of memories –Augusta and Louisa Milman, her sister-in-law Caroline, Louise Diday – as she recognises the same terrible disease; consumption.

1887 was a very difficult year at the nursing home, and March the worst month of all; first of all, their oldest loyal servant and nurse, Esther Elizabeth Rolls, fell ill.

Esther, the "faithful friend and attendant for 30 years[251]," who had cared for Hannah Vincent, Caroline Bonnett, and innumerable ladies of the nursing home, became a patient herself and died from bronchitis on 12th March, aged 74.

At the same time, Emilia's cousin and business partner, Caroline Bonnett, had been in a precarious state of health for some time and at some point during the last few months had lost her mental capacity; or to use the language of the time, she had become a lunatic. This was not a term of abuse; to be a lunatic was to be in need of, and deserving, care and protection.

Following an application to the Lunacy Commission, Caroline was officially declared a lunatic and her sister, Mrs Frances Emily Balston, was appointed her executor. Mrs Balston was thus authorised to make decisions regarding Caroline's financial affairs. Caroline died on 18th March from "cerebral disease;" perhaps epilepsy, a stroke, Parkinson's, or one of the many kinds of dementia[252].

Three days later, on 21st March 1887, Lucy May Owindia died from phthisis – pulmonary tuberculosis – at eight years old[253].

Esther Rolls, Caroline Bonnett and Lucy May Owindia are interred at Reading Old Cemetery, in a plot that was purchased by Emilia, no doubt with the heaviest of hearts[254].

Chapter five: Plans for the future

In 1888, Emilia was 60 years old and the last year had taken its toll. Her own health was becoming a cause for concern and she was planning ahead for retirement.

Emilia had added Croydon Lodge to The Nursing Home's two semi-detached houses, but financial pressures meant that she had, for some periods of time, found tenants for the house. A letter to the *Reading Mercury* in March 1888 explained the situation; her initial strategy had been to take in three patients who paid the full cost of their care, and thus secured the continuance of the home for the benefit of the ladies' whose fees were supplemented. But by March 1888, the three private patients had all died, and the newer patients were all ladies in reduced circumstances[255].

At the same time, she wished to retire, but realising her assets by selling the properties would mean she would have to evict the present residents.

A meeting of nursing home supporters was called; they gathered at the Royal Assembly Rooms in Reading, with Richard Benyon, High Sheriff of Berkshire and former Reading M.P., in the chair. Emilia's brother Thomas came over from Pusey; he had by this time exchanged the demanding role of chaplain at St Mary's Home, Wantage for the more relaxed duties of a country Rector.

The meeting discussed how a permanent committee could take over the work that Emilia started, and how to raise the sum of £2,500 to buy the three houses from her.

Mr. O.C. Maurice began by paying tribute to the home,

"...having been connected with the home ever since Miss Vincent started it and he imagined no one could speak more capably than he of the admirable way in which the institution had been carried on. It was second to none that he knew, both for nursing and the kindness

shown to the patients; and he had the greatest possible pleasure in testifying to the admirable way in which the patients were looked after by the ladies who devoted their time to that work of love[256]."

By the end of the meeting, the new committee had been nominated; Mr. Richard Benyon as president; Right Hon. Sir John Mowbray, Bart., M.P., Mr. G. Mount M.P., Mr. C.T. Murdoch, M.P. and Mr. F. Wilder as vice presidents. Dr. H. French Banham, Mr. F.C.C. Barnett, Mr. W.F. Blandy, Rev. Cecil F.J. Bourke, Rev. Canon Garry, Rev. D.M. Gardner, Dr. J. Illingworth, Rev. F.D. Kiddle, Mr. O.C. Maurice, Mr. S.S. Melville, Mr. Walter Palmer, Rev. Canon Payne, Mr. Thomas Rogers, Mr. F.G. Saunders; with Mr. G.E.B. Rogers as Honorary Secretary.

Chapter six: *Royal patronage and the Helena Nursing Home*

The managing committee decided that their charity needed a patron, and wrote to Queen Victoria's middle daughter, the Princess Helena, known formally as the Princess Christian, since her marriage to Prince Christian of Schleswig-Holstein. The Prince and Princess lived at Cumberland House, near to Windsor Castle, as the Queen wanted them to be near her. The Princess was renowned for her support to charitable causes and as she was particular interested in nursing, she supported hundreds of medically related organisations, including the Red Cross and the British Nurses' Association.

The Nursing Home committee members were delighted when the princess agreed to be their patron, and The Nursing Home at 1 Brownlow Road was accordingly renamed the Helena Nursing Home. With royal interest, fundraising and publicity stepped up a pace.

In January of 1889, Mrs Palmer, the wife of Reading's mayor, George Palmer of the famous Huntley and Palmer's biscuit family, organised a concert, featuring "members of Magdalen College, Oxford and others," held in the New Town Hall, Reading.

Tickets were not cheap; the concert in the morning was more expensive than the evening show, which would have catered for people who had to work during the day;

"Morning concert, 6s, 4s and 2s, with a family ticket for a guinea.
Evening concert, 4s, 2s 6d and 1s, with a family ticket for 15s[257]."

Royal patronage attracted some up-market sponsors; including the Duchess of Wellington, the Marchioness of Ailsa, the Marchioness of Conyngham, the Marchioness of Downshire, the Lady Diana Huddleston, and many more, alongside Emilia's friends and neighbours, Lord Saye and Sele's family; in addition, the well-known notables of Berkshire; including Mr. and Mrs Benyon of Englefield, the Blandys, Simonds, Palmers, and Moncks, Mrs De Vitre from Keep Hatch, Wokingham, and Mrs Walter from Bear Wood, Sindlesham[258]. Later, it was announced that the concert had raised £75[259], almost as much as that year's sale of work, which raised £100.

The nursing home's future was secure. Emilia could start planning her retirement.

There was one more challenge to face before she actually handed over the keys to the Helena Home; an epidemic of influenza.

Chapter seven: Pandemic Influenza

Daniel Ferbridge, a 24-year-old delivery driver, hadn't felt well for a few days, but turned up to work as usual at Mr. Page's bakery in Hambrook Street, Southsea, Hampshire. He was aching all over, and his chest felt bad. He'd seen Dr. Harding in Portsea, but didn't like the medicine he gave him, so stopped taking it. He told his father about his aches and pains, and said he'd rather stay in bed than go to work. But with a pregnant wife at home, and with no recourse to sick pay or state benefits, he had no choice but to soldier on. Besides, he and a lot of other people were used to getting bronchitis every winter, he'd be fine.

At the shop, he loaded up the cart as usual, and was off on his delivery round by quarter to seven. An hour later, he was spotted by an acquaintance, Charles Hayward. The baker's delivery trap was in Melbourne Street, and Dan Ferbridge was sitting in it – but in a very peculiar position. Mr. Hayward smiled and went to wake up his friend.

"Come on, Dan, wake up," he said, "you won't get home tonight if you stay here."

He shook him, then tried to pull him out of his seat. Mr. Hayward then hurried back to his own cart to get a lamp; on closer examination he realised with horror that Dan Ferbridge was dead. Leaving his own cart in the street, Hayward drove the body to Landport Police Station. Dr. Hann, who conducted the post-mortem, discovered pneumonia and congestion of the brain, heart and kidneys[260],[261].

Neighbours and friends rallied around Emily, Daniel's young pregnant widow; there was a collection on her behalf, which raised more than £10[262]. Her son, Frederick Daniel Ferbridge, was born that summer, but sadly, only lived for three months[263].

Daniel Ferbridge was just one of millions of people who died during the forgotten influenza epidemic of 1889-1892.

Could anyone have predicted that in 2020, a novel coronavirus would work itself around the world, causing sickness, death and economic destruction? The truth is, that global pandemics are entirely predictable. They have happened before and will happen again, simply because viruses mutate and as they mutate, they become able to cross from one species to another, mutate some more and cross over some more. It's simply what viruses do. Examples include the pox family, polio, influenza and many more.

In 1889, germ theory was becoming accepted and some bacteria, such as *streptococcus*, were being identified and named. Viruses, too small to be seen, were yet undiscovered.

Modes of transmission of infection were only beginning to be understood. Many doctors still believed in the miasma theory, therefore many illnesses were still being labelled as due to malaria – *mal aria* – bad air. There was no understanding that some illnesses, like malaria (as termed today) and dengue fever were spread by parasites via mosquito bites. Water was not always as clean as it looked, and general cleanliness, especially among the poor, could be difficult to achieve. Quarantining the sick was understood to be effective, but almost impossible to do for most people, especially for the bread-winners of the family, since not working would mean no food for the whole family. Families of the lowest incomes tended to live in overcrowded conditions, perhaps several families to a house, sharing a kitchen and somewhat primitive sanitary arrangements, and social distancing was nigh on impossible.

The pages of *The Lancet* for 1889 and the few years following trace the debate among doctors and scientists.

What was this illness? What was its cause? How was it spread? How best to treat it?

It seems to have started in Russia, as a short article explained in *The Lancet* in November 1889;

"An epidemic of influenza of considerable intensity is at present prevailing at St. Petersburg, causing much inconvenience to business, the stoppage of work in factories, and the disablement of the garrison. It is calculated that between 20% and 30% of the entire population are affected, and comparisons are being made with other epidemics recorded in history. As the tendency of this disease is to become pandemic, it is possible that we may soon hear of its extension to other parts of the continent. The last time it appeared in any marked degree in England was in 1847, when in London alone it was computed that 250,000 persons suffered[264]."

Within a few short weeks, influenza was reported in Vienna, Belgrade, Copenhagen, Brussels, Paris, Birmingham, Dover and London. Among the high-profile victims taking to their beds were the Queen of Sweden and Norway and Monsieur Carnot, president of France.

One early theory was that the epidemic was one of dengue fever, since the main symptoms were fever and headache, accompanied by a running cold[265]. However, Mr. J.O. Hunter, claiming personal experience of epidemics of dengue fever on the West Coast of South America, wrote to *The Lancet* to state that he had never seen it communicated from person to person, and in that, it resembled yellow fever[266]. The missing piece of the puzzle, to go with the observation that these diseases were not spread person to person, would be the discovery that malaria, dengue fever and yellow fever were all being spread by mosquitoes. The yellow fever virus had the honour of being the first human virus to be isolated, in 1927[267].

An interesting theory, from Dr. Germain See in Paris was that influenza was a form of rinderpest (a viral disease usually affecting cattle), and probably originated from cows.[268]

Early speculation was contradictory; it was influenza, it was dengue fever. It was just a cold, and we all know people who exaggerate their symptoms, labelling a cold as influenza. It was sure to lead to cholera or typhus, or even measles; and it wasn't, because these conditions are not related to each other. It was mild and nothing to worry about, and it was very serious. According to Dr. Henry Weekes of Barnstaple, it was caused by earthquakes in Eastern Europe. He stated,

"It reminds me of the results of certain earthquakes in New Zealand some 30 years ago, after which much sickness of a new and depressing nature broke out, especially in the Valley of the Hutt in the Province of Wellington. There is no more difficulty in admitting an atmospheric pollution travelling across the Atlantic to New York than that the red sunsets all round the world were lately caused by the dust of a Java volcano[269]."

Another contributor to *The Lancet* suggested that influenza had arisen first in lambs, then spread to horses, and thence to humans; not for the first time raising the possibility of zoonosis – diseases spreading from species to species[270].

While the medical men debated and argued, most ordinary people had no choice but to continue everyday life, working as usual.

"Christmas Eve in Vienna was passed in gloom, if not in sorrow. It is ordinarily a gay capital at this season, and had nothing untoward happened, its reputation for festivities would not have suffered. But that dreadful influenza has spoiled all the mirth and frolic around the Christmas trees. Parents meet in the street and exchange

sad greetings, for in a large number of cases their children are sufferers from the epidemic and have to be kept in bed[271]."

In Paris, field tents had been erected in the grounds of Beaujon Hospital, to accommodate another 500 patients.[272]

By the end of December 1889, there was no doubt that influenza was in the United Kingdom. Lord Salisbury, the British Prime Minister, was an early casualty[273]. The large number of cases meant widespread disruption to schools and workplaces. Although the illness was mild in most cases, it could also be short, sharp and nasty, the main symptoms being fever and severe muscle pains. Most sufferers recovered within a few days and resumed normal life. However, a large proportion of those affected were ill for a much longer period – similar to the experience of the more recent "Long Covid."

In Brighton, a town which had long attracted a high number of convalescents from many kinds of illness, and therefore tended to accommodate clusters of infection, reported the abnormally high death rate of 60.9 per thousand, which later dropped to near its average, to 24.6[274] (The pre-coronavirus death rate for the UK, in 2019, was 9.25 per thousand[275]).

An increasing number of people were needing hospital treatment for inflammation of the lungs, pleurisy, and peritonitis. Glands were enlarged, there were skin rashes, abdominal pains, sometimes diarrhoea and often pneumonia[276]. Other patients reported a roseola-like rash, loss of appetite, a bitter taste in the mouth and weakness that could last for weeks[277]. Depression was common[278], and a rise in cases of suicide was noted.

In some cases, the suicide could be directly linked to influenza; cases such as Catherine Bradshaw in Bloomsbury who was discovered by her husband lying on the floor with a scarf and some string tight around her neck. She had been suffering from influenza, followed by bronchitis and been very depressed in spirits[279].

In Stamford, housekeeper Sophie Hardy drowned herself in a water cistern, leaving a note that said, "I feel so ill, I can't live like this. My poor head[280]."

John Short, a respected tradesman of Bampton, Devon, cut his own throat with a pocketknife "while of unsound mind induced by illness[281]".

Even a year after suffering, a suicide might be put down to the flu; Mr. William Rickwood, late secretary to the London General Porters' Benevolent Association, hanged himself in his office. His doctor testified at the inquest that "Influenza interfered with the heart's action, and so, by preventing a proper supply of blood to the brain, caused sleeplessness and depression." Mr. Rickwood had left a note, stating,

"Sleeplessness for eight or nine months is the cause of my act. Nothing except this will, I hope, make my life dishonourable[282]."

Early remedies ranged from the slightly useful to the bizarre; quinine, antipyrine, acetanilide and phenacetin (antecedents of paracetamol) were of some use but were not without adverse side-effects. Inhalation therapies such as eucalyptus and menthol might have helped to relieve some of the symptoms. Tartar emetic and James's Powder, or Dr. James's Fever Powder, were popular remedies, but with a main ingredient of antimony, would have done more harm than good.

Dr. T.J. MacLagan in Cadogan Place, London, reported good results from regular, high doses of salicine, a derivative of willow bark, and so far, had not noted serious side-effects, other than temporary deafness[283]. A later formulation of acetylsalicylic acid – aspirin – was safer and available by 1899.

Dr. Richard Sisley of York Street, London, approved quinine, light food and a course of hot sea-water baths, particularly recommending Brighton, Eastbourne, Hastings and Ramsgate[284]. Only the wealthy, of course, could afford the expense of such a holiday, and the transport of a sick person to a seaside resort.

Alcohol had long been a popular remedy for many kinds of complaint; people who could afford it would have been taking regular small amounts of champagne, sherry, brandy and good quality wine. This was even more the case across the Channel; a popular remedy recommended by the *Liberté* was the mixture of ale and stout known in England as half-and-half[285]. Warmed alcohol, usually wine or brandy, was such a popular remedy that 1500 people were arrested in Paris for drunkenness during three days over Christmas, and claimed influenza precautions in their defence.[286]

At the Spring Street Post Office, Paddington, 30 out of 80 postman were ill, inconveniently, in December. Most of them recovered quickly, but one of them stated,

"I was so bad I could scarcely see, and twice my legs gave way whilst I was delivering letters, and I had to go home, and be seen by Dr. Stone. I was away three days, but they had to send for me to go on again on account of the Christmas deliveries."

150 shop assistants were also off work in Westbourne Grove[287].

Many patients reported that the illness overtook them with extraordinary suddenness; a London cabman reported for work and returned his cab within an hour, feeling too ill to continue. An errand boy left home perfectly well, and half an hour after reaching the place where he was employed, fell to the ground with what he described as cramp in his legs, which turned out to be followed by other symptoms of Russian influenza.[288]

By the 1890s, there had been great improvements and strides in knowledge regarding the importance of hygiene and clean water. However, this Reading local reporter may have been a little too optimistic in his assessment of the protection of sanitary precautions from viruses:

"... [influenza] *began in that insanitary country, Russia, and it has spread where defective drainage and short and impure water supplies exist, and where the ordinary rules of sanitary science are neglected. Happily for us, the wisdom of a former generation recognised the necessity for improved sanitary regulations in Reading, and the reward for their thought and labour will be seen in the greater immunity from the epidemic, or in its diminished force should it unfortunately visit our town*[289]."

It was already there. Within days, there were high numbers of absences at the major employers, such as Huntley and Palmer's biscuit factory, the post office, police force and seeds and bulbs producer Sutton and Sons. Quinine was being recommended as a preventive, and so Sutton and Sons distributed at least 500 doses among its employees.[290]

The Deputy Mayor, Mr. George W. Palmer, was ill and confined to his house. At Windsor, cases were reported in the 1st Lifeguards, and the 2nd Battalion Coldstream Guards. At Aldershot, there were many cases both in town and the military camp, and over 100 new patients admitted at the Cambridge hospital in a week[291].

The Helena Home's patron, the Princess Christian, spent much of 1889 in Wiesbaden, Hesse (present-day Germany), where she was receiving treatment for problems with her eyes. In February 1890, news came from Wiesbaden that Princess Christian was suffering from a severe attack of influenza[292].

There was no doubt that people were dying from influenza but counting the dead was a complicated business. The number dying with influenza as the immediate cause was small; but there was a growing awareness that an attack of influenza left the patient vulnerable to subsequent infections.

"Thus, while the deaths in Paris certified as due to influenza were but 213 in all, the general mortality of the city during the months of December and January exceeded the average by no less than 5500, an excess which could not be accounted for by any climactic conditions, an unusual prevalence of other epidemics, or, in fact, by anything except the influence, direct or indirect, of this disease[293]."

Other diseases, such as smallpox, enteric fever, scarlatina, diphtheria, measles and whooping cough were still around and claimed their victims, but;

"A larger proportion than usual of those persons suffering from these diseases succumbed to pulmonary complications. The enormous increase of the mortality from bronchitis, pneumonia, and pleurisy was clearly owing to the frequent occurrence of these conditions as sequelae of previous attacks of influenza; but still more remarkable was the increased mortality from chronic diseases, as phthisis [tuberculosis], organic lesions of the heart, diabetes, alcoholism, chronic diseases of the brain, kidneys &c., in which the supervention of influenza, even of a mild or obscure type, hastened a fatal termination, and not infrequently suddenly....[294]"

It was not generally dangerous to children,

"unless already suffering from pulmonary affections, or diseases, such as measles and whooping cough, and liable to pulmonary complications, and with these exceptions it was rarely fatal to persons under 20 years of age... It was only half as fatal to women as to men...."

The impact of depression was sadly reflected in an increase in suicides; an increase of about 40% was reported in Paris.[295]

Mr. Reginald Noott, assistant medical officer at the state criminal lunatic asylum, Broadmoor, Berkshire, contributed his experience to *The Lancet*. At the time, Broadmoor housed 416 male patients and 151 female patients, along with 84 male attendants and 34 female attendants.

Between January and May 1890, 206 individuals were ill, mostly exhibiting the classic symptoms of fever, headache, muscular pains, depression and loss of appetite. Among the patients, who were already mentally ill, the symptoms of depression tended to be much worse, in one case a "condition of complete mental torpor which lasted four weeks."

Three of the inmates developed pneumonia and died.

Broadmoor in those days accommodated children as well as adults. Mr. Noott's observation was that "generally, it was noticed that it [the epidemic] attacked adults much more than children, that as a rule the older the patient the more severe were the symptoms[296]."

The Russian Influenza returned for three successive winters. In January 1892, it took its highest profile victim; Prince Albert Victor, Duke of Clarence and Avondale, eldest son of the Prince of Wales, the future King Edward VII. It was a terrible shock after a short illness, and at the age of only 28. Nicknamed "Eddy" by his family, the prince had been born prematurely, and was said not to have had a strong constitution. His death, before his father and grandmother, changed history and the line of royal succession. His fiancée, Princess Mary of Teck, later married his younger brother, who became King George V in 1910.

By this time, influenza had visited many of the notable houses of Berkshire; Maiden Erlegh, Coombe Park, Swallowfield Park, Wasing House, Sulhamstead House, Crookham House, Calcot Park, Culverlands, Wokefield Park, Burghfield Manor, Sulham, Englefield and Caversham Park. At Erlegh Whiteknights, Mr. and Mrs Porter and several servants took to their beds. Mr. Martin Hope Sutton of Cintra Lodge[297] had also been ill.

At Bill Hill House, Hurst, near Wokingham, Captain James Edward Leveson-Gower, died aged 65.[298] At Burghfield, Mr. Thomas Bland Garland, J.P., who had donated the collections that formed the nucleus of Reading Museum, already had problems with his liver. He died following influenza in February 1892[299].

Reading's M.P., Mr. Charles Townsend Murdoch was reported in January 1892 to be recovering from influenza and hopeful of making a convalescent journey to Europe[300]; but in April, he was still unwell, and exhausted from making the journey to Cannes; however, he eventually reached his destination, Milan, in Italy, by making his journey in easy stages[301].

We can only guess as to how much the Victorian belief in the warmer climates of Europe as a curative contributed to the spread of the viral illness along the tourist routes.

At the Reading Workhouse in Oxford Road, most of the inmates had been ill, and with no such recourse to a milder climate. Dr. Battiss was reported to have seen 1,000 patients in a week. The Friendly Societies which provided medical benefits, for example the Hearts of Oak Benefit Society, the Oddfellows, Foresters, and Sons of Temperance, found themselves overwhelmed by applicants[302]. The *Reading Mercury* found it worthy of note that there were now five full-time gravediggers employed at the cemetery, and a high number of funerals; 54 in the first week of the year. On two occasions there had been 11 funerals in one day, and two occasions of the funerals of married couples.

It was well-known that the quarantining of sufferers of many diseases helped reduce the spread of infection, but there appears to have been little more than token efforts at social distancing.

The *Reading Mercury* reported the sad deaths of three small children of P.C. George Gould, who all died on the same day from bronchitis following influenza. In the very same column, it reports on an evening of very pleasant entertainment at the workhouse (that same workhouse where most of the inmates were or had been ill), thanks to the members and friends of the Reading United Mission Choir. Once the choir had entertained in the main hall, they proceeded to the sick ward and sang several pieces there[303].

The population of Reading at that time was 60,054 and 1,094 deaths had occurred in the Borough during 1891. Causes of death included scarlatina, measles, diphtheria, whooping cough, typhoid fever, diarrhoea, puerperal fever, phthisis, heart disease and injuries. 39 deaths were attributed directly to influenza, but no doubt some of the other deaths, especially the 187 deaths attributed to bronchitis, pneumonia and pleurisy had influenza as a contributing factor[304].

Throughout the three years when the influenza epidemic did its worst in Reading, Emilia Vincent's problems were like those of any care home manager today. The need to care for vulnerable residents, and protect them from infection (when some of them do not understand the need for extra hygiene), and at the same time to try to keep their lives as normal as possible; the continuing challenge of covering shifts when more staff are falling ill every day, or reluctant to work because they fear becoming ill, or conversely, turning up for work when they are not fit, is one that I know well; along with the concerns of how the tasks of shopping, activities, entertainments, cleaning, and more cleaning get done in the face of additional risk assessments, increased precautions for staff, and the isolation of residents who are ill.

There is no information regarding the Helena Nursing Home for the first two years of the epidemic; but the winters of 1891-2, and 1892-3, at least, were difficult ones and this is reflected in the information we can glean from Emilia's appeal letters to the local press.

By this time, the home had been in existence for 13 years. A total of nearly 50 patients had been cared for, and 21 had died from various conditions, including nine from cancer.

Emilia's appeals from this period mention the struggles during the pandemic, including this letter from June 1892;

"We have lost many kind friends and supporters during the past year. I am therefore most anxious to enlist the sympathy of new residents in Reading and the neighbourhood. Our funds are nearly exhausted. They were heavily taxed during the influenza epidemic, when we had to seek much extra help to supply the place of nurses and servants suddenly turned into extra patients[305]."

The following winter was again difficult; in December 1892, the 14th anniversary of the Helena Nursing Home was celebrated as usual, but the arrangements had to be different. There was Holy Communion at All Saints' Church at 8am, for friends and supporters, and in the afternoon a Thanksgiving service at the home's chapel for patients and workers. The Bishop of Reading gave an address and visited some of the patients. In normal years, the annual sale of work would have taken place in the home and garden. This year however,

"...on account of the many serious cases of illness in the home it was impossible to have the annual sale on the premises. Mr. Blandy, in consequence, kindly lent a room in his house in Downshire Square. Many pretty and useful articles were sent, in addition to the warm clothing made in the home." [306]

The annual sale of work was the major fundraiser of the year, when it was hoped to raise a substantial amount of the funding needed to support the patients, most of whom did not pay more than one third of the cost of their care. That year, £95 was raised, less than usual. The ladies who came to help included Mrs and the Misses Collins, Mabel and Beatrice Blandy, Emily Morris, Miss Maurice, Miss Smith and Emilia's nieces, the Misses Bedford and Emilia Margaret Vincent[307].

Influenza or coronavirus?

An interesting question was raised comparatively recently; could the influenza epidemic of the 1890s have been a coronavirus?

Coronaviruses came to the world's attention with the SARS (severe acute respiratory syndrome) epidemic which began in 2002, but they have been around for a very long time, and have been studied more in veterinary than in human medicine. There are many different coronaviruses, which infect nearly every kind of creature. In humans, the illnesses are usually mild, and on the level of a common cold or similar. At the same time, it is also known that infectious diseases caused by bacteria, viruses or parasites that infect one kind of animal have regularly jumped to other species; familiar names include ebola, salmonella, the pox family, common colds and influenza and of course, coronaviruses.

A study in 2005 explored a possible link between the influenza epidemic of the 1890s and pleuropneumonia in cattle, which had been devastating cattle farms worldwide since the 1850s. It was highly infectious, and had been controlled by culling herds and restricting movements of cattle. In time it was thought to have been caused by the bacterium *mycoplasma mycoides mycoides*. However, the symptoms, a dry cough with fever and loss of appetite were very similar to those caused by the influenza that arose in St. Petersburg a few years later.

An interesting hypothesis was put forward by Vijgen et al, a group of scientists who published their paper in 2005. In examining the genome of a human coronavirus and a related bovine coronavirus, they proposed that a common ancestor of both could be traced to around 1890[308].

That influenza returned for three winters, then seemed to decrease in intensity. As "herd immunity" developed in the general population, the illness became less significant, though this was at the cost of the deaths and long-term health issues it left in its wake. If any descendant of this same influenza is still with us, we are likely to experience it as a nuisance, just a cold.

At the time of writing, we can be hopeful that Covid-19 will eventually fade into the background; perhaps we can also be hopeful that we will have learned something for the next time.

Chapter eight: A Royal visit

1893 was a year of changes and excitement.

There was sadness too, as one of Emilia's longest-standing residents, Mrs Sarah Bryan, died in the September, aged 82. The cause of her death, certified by Dr. Oliver Calley Maurice, was "Decay of Nature" – old age. Nurse Hester Beasley was caring for her when she died [309]. Hester was a local girl; her father and brothers worked in one of Reading's brick kilns [310].

It was the year that Miss Vincent formally retired and Miss Wate, the first paid Lady-in-Charge, took over the running of the Helena Nursing Home.

By the winter of that year, conditions were back to normal. The Princess Christian had long recovered from her brush with influenza and was back to work – supporting and encouraging her many charitable causes. This was the year she decided to visit the Helena Nursing Home in Reading.

The information regarding her royal visit to Reading and the Helena Home has been compiled from the reports in the *Reading Mercury* and *Berkshire Chronicle* of 25th November 1893.

The 23rd November 1893 was a clear, cold day, and the streets of Reading were lined with crowds of onlookers hoping for a glimpse of Queen Victoria's middle daughter, on her first official visit to Reading.

Many of the town's businesses had been decorated for the occasion, the most spectacular being the jewellers, Messrs Bracher and Sydenham's. The Wellington club was gaily bedecked with flags, and Castle Street and Bath Road stood out as the most noticeable in the way of decoration.

Messrs Brinkworth's display in Castle Street included an exhibition of about 300 cases of seeds and seed potatoes, which the firm were about to send to His Excellency the president of the Zulu Republic.[311]

The Princess Christian of Schleswig-Holstein travelled by train from Windsor to Slough, where the royal saloon carriage was attached to the scheduled 1:35 pm train from Paddington. Her Royal Highness was attended by lady-in-waiting Miss Emily Loch, Colonel Gordon and Mr. Charles Townshend Murdoch, Reading's former M.P. (Mr. Murdoch had made his own recovery from influenza, and returned from his trip to Italy). After reaching the down station at Reading, the saloon carriage was backed to the up platform by a pilot engine and the royal party alighted from the train, to the accompaniment of the band of the 49th Regimental District, under the command of Colonel Borrett, playing the National Anthem. The party was greeted by the Mayor and Mayoress, Mr. and Mrs Charles Gyningham Field. Their 11-year-old daughter, Muriel, curtseyed beautifully and presented the Princess a bouquet of orchids, cattleyas, odontoglossums, with vancratiums, asparagus plumosa and green ferns. The bouquet, in a silver-gilt holder, was supplied by local firm Sutton and Sons, the Queen's seedsmen.

The Great Western Railway's Mr. James W. Gibbs, Divisional Superintendent at Reading, was in charge of the train. Reading station scrubbed up well, under the supervision of Station Master Mr. Fraser and Mr. Hirons the chief clerk; the platform was red-carpeted for the day, and special seating was installed for the comfort of the royal visitor and party.

Reading's town officers formed the welcoming committee: Mr. W.G. Mount, M.P., and Mrs Mount, Mr. P. Wroughton, M.P. and Mrs Wroughton, George William

Palmer, Reading's current M.P. and Mrs Palmer, Mrs Murdoch, Lady Stapleton, Miss Stapleton, Colonel Mande, Colonel and Mrs Borrett, Major and Mrs Mackenzie Edwards, Colonel Gordon and eminent physician, Mr. Oliver Calley Maurice.

Outside the station, the crowds cheered and waved hats and handkerchiefs as Her Royal Highness came into view and was handed into a carriage lent by Mr. and Mrs Benyon of Englefield.

The Royal Berkshire Yeomanry formed a guard of honour under the command of Lieutenant Roberts and Quartermaster Ayres, and accompanied the procession to the town hall, where the 1st Volunteer Battalion Royal Berkshire Regiment were under the command of Captain Louis de L. Simonds, Captain J.C. Blandy and Lieutenant Arthur S. Cooper. The police, including mounted officers, were under the command of Head Constable Tewsley. Her Royal Highness arrived at the Town Hall, where the entrance had been carpeted in crimson, and proceeded to the council chamber.

Local florist Mrs Phippen had provided decorations of shrubs, evergreens and flowers, and the officials, politicians, magistrates and influential ladies watched as the Princess took her place on a raised dais alongside the Mayor.

Among the assembled officials, members of council, and borough magistrates, were Lady Wantage, Lady Russell, Mr. J.O. Griffiths Q.C. (the Recorder), Mr. J.W. Martin (the former Mayor and nursing home neighbour in Brownlow Road), Mr. and Mrs George Palmer, Mr. W.S. Darter, Alderman and Miss Simonds, Alderman Hill, Alderman Messer, the Headmaster of Reading School and Mrs Barnard, Mr. and Mrs W.F. Blandy, Mr. and Mrs Nalder Clark, Alderman and Mrs Andrews, Councillor and Mrs W. Ferguson, Alderman and Mrs Beale, the Clerk of the Peace and Mrs and Miss

Sherwood, Councillor Dodd, Councillor and Mrs D.
Heelas, Mr. J.A. Brain and Miss Brain, Councillor Mrs
Rayment, Mr. and Mrs G. Gilligan, Councillor and Mrs
Waite, Mr. W. Weedon (borough coroner), Miss Alice
Sutton, Miss Ellen Sutton, Mrs Stevens, Councillor and
Mrs Creed, Councillor and Mrs Euerby, Mrs J.R. Cook,
Miss Day, Alderman and Mrs Monck, Councillor and Mrs
Pegler, Councillor and Mrs Cox, Councillor and Mrs
Joseph Milsom, Mrs Wellman, Councillor Wellman,
Alderman and Mrs J.D. Brown, Councillor and Mrs
Poulton, Councillor and Mrs Jackson, Councillor and Mrs
Parfitt, Councillor and Mrs Ernest Simmons, Councillor
and Mrs Hodder, Councillor and Mrs W.H. Simonds,
Alderman and Mrs Blandy, Mr. and Mrs Charles Smith,
Mr. T.L. Walford (J.P.) and Miss Walford, Councillor
Brinn, Councillor Apsley Smith, Councillor G.W. Webb,
Councillor Ridley, Councillor Deverel, and Councillor
Philbrick.

The town clerk, Mr. Henry Day, read an address
which had been handsomely illuminated and embossed
on vellum, and bound in scarlet morocco by Mr. H.E.
Greenslade of the King's Road, Reading:

*"To Her Royal Highness the Princess Helena Augusta
Victoria, Princess Frederick Christian of Schleswig-
Holstein.*

May it please your Royal Highness,

*We, the mayor, aldermen and burgesses of the
Borough of Reading, in the County of Berkshire, desire
most respectfully to approach your Royal Highness and to
offer you a hearty welcome upon this the first occasion on
which we have had the honour of receiving your Royal
Highness in this ancient and loyal borough.*

*We remember with pleasure that your Royal Highness
and your beloved family have long been residents in the
Royal County of Berkshire, and we rejoice to acknowledge*

that it has been the delight of your Royal Highness to devote yourself to works of benevolence and to other objects designed for the social and moral well-being of the people.

It is a matter of special gratification to us, as it will be a pleasure to your Royal Highness that the object of your present visit to this borough is to help forward the beneficent work of extending aid to the ladies, who, suffering from incurable maladies, and especially in the later stages of their illness, need comforts, nursing and care which they or their relatives are without means of sufficiently providing for them.

We earnestly pray Almighty God long to preserve your Royal Highness, still to adorn your exalted position by a life of active benevolence, and that you and your beloved husband and children may continue to be blessed with a large measure of health and happiness.

We beg your Royal Highness to convey to our gracious sovereign (whom may God long preserve) the renewed assurances of our loyalty and attachment towards Her Majesty and her royal house.

Given under our common seal this 23rd day of November 1893.

Chas. G. Field, Mayor,
Henry Day, Town Clerk"

After this welcoming address, the Princess and her party left the council chamber for the New Town Hall, just down the corridor, where she was met by the Helena Nursing Home bazaar committee; Lord Saye and Sele, Rev. Canon Garry, Mr. F.N.A. Garry, Mr. O.C. Maurice, Mr. F.C.C. Barnett, Mr. S.S. Melville, Dr. Marriott, Rev. G.P. Crawfurd, Mr. G.E.B. Rogers (Honorary Secretary); they were joined by the vicar of St. Lawrence, Rev. J.M.

Guilding, the vicar of St. Giles, Rev. J.P. Farler, Colonel Makins M.P. and Mr. J.H. Blagrave. Mr. Strickland, the organist of St. Mary's Church, played the national anthem.

The Rev. Canon Garry offered an opening prayer, and then welcomed the Princess on behalf of the friends of the Helena Nursing Home, and of the three ancient parish churches of Reading.

When Canon Garry had finished his speech, Mr. O.C. Maurice then gave a short history of the home. He outlined how Miss Emilia Vincent had started the home in a small house, with three patients, having previously done similar work at St. Mary's Home.

"I have had the privilege of being the honorary medical officer to the home during that time; and I may say that no one, not even my friend Canon Garry, who so frequently visits it, can have had so good an opportunity as myself of judging of the excellence of its work. Miss Vincent has during the whole of that time devoted her life to the good of the patients, tending them with loving care and tenderness, and aiding the home also very materially by her liberality with her purse."

He paid tribute to the generosity of the sponsors who had raised the funds to enable a committee to purchase the houses, so that the work could continue on a permanent footing. Two donors are singled out for mention; Mr. Richard Benyon, High Steward of the borough, who donated £500, and the late Mr. Thomas Rogers, uncle to the current honorary secretary of the home, whose executors had donated £100.

Mr. Maurice also paid tribute to Miss Emily Morris,

"...who has during the greater part of the time assisted Miss Vincent with the same loving care and tenderness, and whose work, like that of Miss Vincent, has been beyond all praise... I am proud to claim her among my

warmest friends, and to testify to the excellent work she has done for this home."

The Princess Christian then declared the bazaar open, and was conducted around the stalls by Canon Garry, to the accompaniment of an organ recital by Mr. Strickland. During the bazaar, organ recitals were also given by Mr. J.C.B. Tirbutt, organist of All Saints' Church, Mr. F. Davis, organist of St. Giles' Church, and Mr. Chandler, organist of St. Paul's church, Wokingham.

The arrangements for the bazaar this year were rather more grand than usual; Messrs Holmes and Son had erected and fitted the stalls, which had arched trelliswork facades, enamelled white, and draped alternately with pink and pale blue.

The ladies of the home's committee presided over the stalls; Lady Saye and Sele, Mrs Benyon from Englefield and Mrs Walter from Bearwood, Sindlesham, took charge of the Helena Nursing Home stall. Other stalls were in the care of Mrs G.W. Palmer, Lady Wantage, Mrs Murdoch and Mrs John Hargreaves; Mrs Foster and Mrs Storer (flowers, very bright and attractive); Mrs Radcliffe and Miss Noble (pottery); Mrs Crawshay; Miss Blagrave (large number of Viennese articles); Mrs Barnard, Miss Pollard and Miss Maurice; Mrs Melville, Mrs F.C.C. Barnett, and Mrs Francis N.A. Garry (objects of interest from Madeira), Mrs Louis de L. Simonds and Miss Ellen Simonds.

A stall that attracted particular interest was the working dairy stall, of which Mrs Martin J. Sutton was in charge. At this stall, a number of ladies were demonstrating a Victorian hobby which seems to have been short lived; that of churning butter which was then artistically sculpted. The process of churning was under the direction of Miss Estcourt, assisted by some young ladies, dressed in Normandy peasant costumes; Miss Bradshaw, Miss Hart-Davis, Miss Winifred Seaton, Miss

Dora Owen, Miss Laura Colette, and Miss Kathleen Sutton. Her Royal Highness was especially intrigued by the new disc churn, which could produce butter in three minutes, and she even requested Mr. Sutton, who was explaining its operation, to provide her with written instructions which she could forward to her sister, the Empress Frederick of Germany, who was just starting a dairy at her new castle at Kronthal near Homburg. Afterwards at the reception in the council chamber, Mrs Sutton presented the Princess with a beautiful basket of flowers, artistically modelled in butter by Miss Heath, for presentation to the Queen.

Since this was the time before electricity supply to every building could be taken for granted, the newspaper reports also noted that the bazaar was elegantly lighted by electricity. The temporary electric lamps were fitted by Messrs Williams and Sons, of London Street, Reading, and the current was supplied by the Reading Electric Supply Company.

The Café Chantant

The Old Town hall was the setting for the Café Chantant, tastefully decorated and carpeted and arranged with small tables for the visitors to enjoy refreshments and a concert. The small tables and other furniture and carpets in the hall had been furnished by Messrs Holmes and Son. The carpet for the platform, the princess's room and anteroom, and the princess's chair were kindly lent by Messrs Blowers and Son, including a Chesterfield sofa, oak screens and various floral arrangements.

The Reading Mercury and *The Berkshire Chronicle*, give slightly different lists of participants; there may have been last minute changes, or perhaps the programme varied over the two days. There would have been intense competition for who would perform on the first day, when the Princess was in attendance!

The programme of entertainment included:

Dramatic sketch - Miss Frankland and the Earl of Yarmouth

Pianoforte solo – Sturmmarsch – Lizt – Mr. Liebich

Song – Hon. Mrs Sclater-Booth

Mandoline and Guitar Band – Mary – N. Pieraccini

On mandolins; Miss V. Hargreaves, Miss Makins, Miss Cammell and Miss Dryland; and on guitars, Miss Beauchamp, Miss Thoyts, Miss Sutton, Miss Morris, Miss Sydenham and Miss Cammell.

Song – The Requital – Blementhal – Rev. C.A. Treherne

Song – Regret – Cowen – Miss Maurice

Violin solo – Andante and Finale from "Concerto in D minor" – Wieniawski – Mr. Frederiksen

Song – When the Heart – D. Buck – Miss Bayley Harris

Song – Le Jardin – Reber – Miss Brakspear

Mandolin and Guitar Band – La Czarine – L. Ganne

Pianoforte solo – Ballade – Chopin – Mr. Liebich

Song and Dance – Doddle, doddle – Miss Frankland and the Earl of Yarmouth

Song – Mr. James

Vocal duet – Il Tempo – Gabuzzi – The Misses Witherington

Song – Wondering – Moir – Mrs Farler

Pianoforte and violin duo – Sonata – Grieg – Mr. Liebich and Mr. Frederiksen

Song – Lullaby – Brahms – Miss Witherington

Song – He that loves a rosy cheek – Benson – Rev. C.A. Treherne

Song – Mr. James

Song – The Letter Song – Planquette – Miss Bayley-Harris

The *Reading Mercury* additionally lists songs by Madame Jutta Bell, Mr. G. Aspinall, Mr. W. Ford, Mr. D. Bispham and the Rev. F.M. Hargreaves. Madame Bell and Mr. Aspinall also sang duets.

The accompanist was Mr. E.K. Deacon, organist of St. Lawrence's Parish Church

The Princess visits the home

Shortly after half-past three, the Princess and party left the Town Hall for Brownlow Road by way of Friar Street, West Street, Oxford Road, Russell Street, Baker Street, Prospect Street, and Tilehurst Road. It would seem however, that something did not go according to plan; since *The Berkshire Chronicle* then reports;

"In our last week's issue, we gave our readers the best information we could get of the route the procession would take, but we were not furnished by the committee of the council having charge of the arrangements with the official notice, and we cannot congratulate them on the methods they took to convey information to the public, nor on the decorations they displayed on the official portion of the route."

The Princess was accompanied by the Mayor and Mayoress, Mr. G.W. Palmer, MP, and Mrs Palmer; Mr. and Mrs Murdoch, Colonel Gordon, Mrs Benyon and Lady Russell, with the carriages carefully coordinated so that the reception committee arrived at the home first in order to receive the Princess at the door.

Along the railings in the playground of All Saints' School, next door to the home, a number of the pupils were eagerly waiting, each carrying a little flag; and as the Princess passed they waved their flags and cheered. The outside of the home was decorated with brightly coloured bunting.

Some of the young ladies of Wilton House School, a private school in Tilehurst Road, Reading, just around the corner from the home, were waiting at the front door to present another bouquet to the princess.

In the hall of the home, she was welcomed by Lady Stapleton, Mrs Benyon, the Mayor, Mr. and Mrs G.W. Palmer, Mr. and Mrs Murdoch, Lord Saye and Sele, Canon Garry (Honorary Chaplain), Mr. S.S. Melville of Star Mead, Wokingham (Honorary Treasurer), Dr. Charles Marriott (Honorary Physician), Mr. Oliver Calley Maurice (Honorary Surgeon), Captain A. Tupman, and Mr. G.E.B. Rogers, Honorary Secretary to the committee.

Also waiting was Miss Wate, the lady appointed to take over from Emilia Vincent; she was the first paid matron of the home.

Miss Wate showed the Princess Helena around the house and introduced her to the residents. Her Royal Highness seemed very pleased with her tour of the buildings, and impressed with the homely appearance and privacy of the 12 individual bedsitting rooms.

After some private business in the town, Her Royal Highness returned to Windsor in the royal saloon carriage, which was now attached to the 5:35 pm train, and was again heartily cheered by a crowd of spectators at the town hall and railway station.

The bazaar continued the following day and was opened by Lady Wantage, who was presented with a bouquet by the Mayor of Reading's younger daughter, eight-year-old Lilian Simpson Field.

Later that evening, those of the Yeomanry who formed the escort for Princess Christian were generously entertained to dinner at the George Hotel. Lieutenant Roberts presided, quartermaster Giles Ayres being the vice-chair. They toasted the Princess's health and Mr. F. Davis presided at the piano for some community singing.

The Reading Mercury adds a note concerning police presence on the day; in addition to officers and the six mounted police keeping an eye on the crowds, Detective Sergeant McCarthy from Scotland Yard was in attendance. D.S. McCarthy personally apprehended a man named Mason, who was attempting to pick pockets near the station. In the hall itself during Thursday's proceedings, several ladies had their pockets picked.

The fundraising efforts of 1893 greatly surpassed any previous year's efforts; the presence of Princess Helena, her entourage, and the additional sponsorship and custom attracted by royal patronage had paid off. Even after paying for some professional services to achieve the standards expected, the two days raised the staggering sum of just over £662[312].

Sadly, though Emilia had done much of the work in preparation for this major event in the life of the nursing home, she herself was not able to attend the bazaar due to illness.

Princess Helena did not visit the home again, but royal involvement continued. In 1899, the home received a personal gift from Queen Victoria herself; Her Majesty sent a scarf she had personally knitted. This item was not sold, but framed, and hung for many years in the entrance hall of the Helena Nursing Home[313].

Part four; retirement

Chapter one; Lynton

Emilia retired and left the running of the Helena Nursing Home to its management committee, headed by the very capable Mrs Benyon, who continued in the role for many years.

There was, for the first time, a paid Lady-in-Charge, Miss Wate.

Miss Morris, who had acted as Emilia's secretary, remained involved with the home for several more years; she was a member of the committee that took over the management of the home [314], [315], and stepped in as Lady-in-Charge when Miss Wate became ill.

Emilia had not gone far; she moved across the road to Lynton, a house built in a similar style to the old Croydon Lodge (North House).

At least two other ladies lived there with her; Rosa de Pothonier, who had first visited Emilia at Jesse Terrace in 1881, and Miss Mary Prescott.

It is not known why Rosa wished to continue to live with Emilia, or why Emilia still wished to be responsible for Rosa's care. In any event, Rosa remained with Emilia at Lynton until her death in 1894. She was interred at Reading Cemetery in the same plot as three people special to Emilia; Esther Rolls, Caroline Bonnett and Lucy May Owindia. Emilia herself had paid for this burial plot, after that terrible week in March 1887 when Esther, Caroline and Lucy all died. Esther had been a family servant for 30 years; Caroline was her cousin, and Lucy a child left in her care. Was Rosa simply interred in a space that was available? Or had she become, over the years, a close friend and someone for whom Emilia felt a special responsibility? I would love to know.

Miss Mary Prescott

Mary Prescott was the newcomer to Brownlow Road; she had lived in India for many years, where she taught in a girls' school in Bombay (renamed Mumbai in 1995), Miss Prescott's Fort Christian School. In her school, girls of all nationalities were taught together; sadly, that was not the norm at the time. Miss Prescott worked in the school for many years at nominal remuneration, and personally raised £600 from her friends in England for the school's redevelopment fund[316]. The school moved to a new site on the esplanade, Bombay, and renamed the Frere-Fletcher School. It included provision for 25 girls to board, with priority given to orphans[317]. The school was renamed again in 1915, and became the J.B. Petit School for Girls, which remains its name to this day.

Somewhere around 1890, Miss Prescott returned to England and lived for a short time in Bath before moving to live with Emilia at Lynton.

There was some personal connection with Emilia's family – she named Emilia's cousin, Mrs Frances Emily Balston and Emilia's nephew, Mr. Charles Greaves Vincent, as her executors, and left her small estate to Mrs Balston. Miss Prescott died at Lynton in 1896 at the age of 82.

In St. Thomas Cathedral, Mumbai, there is a brass memorial plaque, with the words;

---

*"Sacred to the memory of
Mary Prescott,
One of the benefactors of the Frere-
Fletcher School (1872-1890)*

*Died at Reading, England, 18 December
1896.*

*Erected by a few friends and former
pupils[318].*

Chapter two; Clevedon, Somerset

Early in the twentieth century, Emilia moved to Clevedon, Somerset, the fashionable seaside town where her brother, Rev. Thomas Vincent, had retired, and where his wife, Dora, had died in 1898. Their sons, George and Thomas Augustine had emigrated to the U.S.A. some years previously. Thomas and his daughter, Dorothea, lived at Hillsborough, St. John's Road, and Emilia took three rooms not far away, at 6 St. John's Avenue.

While there, she sorted out some of her own affairs, including making a will in 1906, and adding a codicil later in the year.

Thomas lived to the age of 88, and died at Hillsborough, cared for by Dorothea, in 1908. The cause of his death is given as "old age, syncope [which means fainting][319]."

After Thomas' death, Emilia moved to Winchester, to an up-market apartment in a house in St. Cross Road, for reasons unknown.

Dorothea Vincent, having dutifully cared for her father until the end of his life, subsequently married the Rev. Herbert Claud Muriel, and lived at Marseilles, then Bordighera, Italy, where Mr. Muriel was Anglican chaplain throughout the Great War.

By 1911, Emilia was back in Reading, taking three rooms at 73 London Road, with a live-in nurse, Harriet Kate Geary, who had worked for her at the Helena Nursing Home[320]. In the end, Emilia passed the last years of her life as a well-off person expected – at home, cared for by paid staff.

Another of her carers was Mrs Elizabeth Luke, who was present when Emilia died on 16th December, 1913, aged 85, from a cerebral haemorrhage. Mrs Luke's address on Emilia's death certificate is given as 171 London Road, and she appears in available censuses as a nurse.[321]

Emilia left an estate of more than £12,000, which was mostly divided among her nieces and nephews. Among her other legacies was £100 each for the Helena Nursing Home and St. Mary's Home in Reading. Her faithful companion and nurse, Harriet Kate Geary, received £200, a silver watch and her clothes. Her executors were her nephew, Charles Greaves Vincent and niece, Georgina Mary Bedford[322].

It's fitting that Emilia's last home, a handsome four-storey semi-detached house, opposite the Royal Berkshire Hospital in London Road, Reading, is now a G.P.'s surgery.

Figure 17; 73 London Road, Reading, July 2021.
Photo by Kim Tame

Chapter three; The Helena Home After Emilia

The Princess Christian died in 1923 and was buried in St. George's Chapel, Windsor. Her daughter, Princess Helena Victoria, who had increasingly taken on her mother's duties as she became older, became patron of the Helena Nursing Home.

In 1930, Her Highness The Dowager Ranee of Sarawak (Margaret, Lady Brooke), was one of the home's vice-presidents. Sarawak is a state of Malaysia which came under British control in 1839, when James Brooke, a British sailor, helped to quell a rebellion against Sultan Omar Ali Saifuddin II. Brooke became governor of Sarawak, and the family later became known as the White Rajahs. All three White Rajahs — James Brooke, Charles Brooke and Charles Vyner de Windt Brooke — are buried at Sheepstor, Dartmoor, at St. Leonard's Church.

The Helena Nursing Home continued to be supported by its committee of wealthy supporters, comprised of a later generation of Benyons, Simonds, and the Saye and Sele family.

The 1930 report lists some improvements to the home; four rooms redecorated, a new vegetable and dry goods store, the boiler house enlarged to form a drying room. It was hoped that the dampness in the wall of the maids' sitting room would now improve. Miss Stacey, a current patient, had donated a moveable garden shelter.

The home still cared for ladies suffering from a great variety of conditions;

Neurotic paralysis, arthritis, sclerosis of spinal nerves, disseminated sclerosis, arterio-sclerosis, heart disease, peptic ulcer and four ladies with rheumatoid arthritis. One lady had been in residence for 30 years.

The report also lists the home's subscribers; raising a total of £217 15s 6d in regular subscriptions in 1930, and one-off donations of £27 18s 6d. Smaller sums, raised by the Helena Home Helpers' League amounted to £34 2s.

The annual sale of work that year raised the sum of £516 19s 6d. The home was wealthy enough that year to hold a reserve fund of almost £7,000, held in stocks and shares. The home's expenses amounted to nearly £2,040, towards which the patients themselves had paid just over £758, the remainder of their care being paid for by fundraising and donations[323].

In 1954, the home was still receiving regular support from the community; including books, garden produce, and the donations from church and school harvest festivals. There was an annual jumble sale, which that year had paid for a new carpet for the sitting room. The home had a lift! It was operated manually, and the committee was hoping to raise enough funds to install an electric version. The bed-sitting rooms now had gas-fires, and the communal sitting room had television and wireless[324].

Home for Clergy Widows

In 1958, the Helena Nursing Home passed into the hands of the Church of England Pensions Board and became a home for the widows of clergymen. It was renamed "Helena House" and provided subsidised accommodation for 17 ladies.

A Cause for Concern/Prospects

At length, Helena House once again came to the end of its usefulness for its then occupants; in 1979, the home was bought by a new charity headed by Baptist minister

David Potter and his wife Madeleine, inspired by their experience with their daughter Rachel, who had Downs Syndrome. They were looking for a permanent home for Rachel, but did not find anything that suited her needs and their values.

Helena House was refurbished, and the first three residents with learning disabilities moved in, in 1982[325]. The new charity was called A Cause for Concern, later renamed Prospects for People with Learning Difficulties. A new community formed, and up to 19 residents lived at Helena House until the home closed in 2013. The residents of that time moved to 34 St. Ronan's Road, Reading.

Helena House was sold and redeveloped; it was converted into flats and North House, the former Croydon Lodge, into a house of multiple occupancy. Part of the ground floor of Helena House, two rooms that have variously been bedrooms, a lounge and offices, was demolished to allow the creation of a parking area at the rear.

Prospects subsequently merged with another Christian provider of care, Livability, who continued at St Ronan's Road until 2021.

Epilogue

Emilia's last resting place is among the trees and lush green grass of Reading cemetery. At the junction of two main roads, named, of course, Cemetery Junction, there is always some traffic noise, but this is a peaceful place, nonetheless. Emilia lies among friends; former residents and supporters, nurses and servants, sleep amid wild flowers, birdsong, mature trees and shrubbery, and the resident rabbits and deer.

Her grave is marked with a long, low stone shaped like a cross, and there is the simple inscription; "Emilia Vincent. A life devoted to others."

Figure 18; Emilia Vincent's grave (centre) at Reading old cemetery.
Photo by Kim Tame

References, sources and acknowledgements

This has been a fascinating journey of discovery, assisted by visits to the places where Emilia has lived, and the huge amount of information that is freely or cheaply available online. As I was researching and writing through the Covid-19 lockdown periods of 2020 and 2021, the amount of material available from my desk is amazing and deeply appreciated.

Newspapers

Most of the newspaper references have come from the British Newspaper Archive; www.britishnewspaperarchive.co.uk (with subscription)

For The Times and The Guardian; www.newspapers.com (with subscription)

For Australian newspapers; https://trove.nla.gov.au/ (free of charge)

Family information

This kind of research is not cheap, but it's worth ordering all the certificates and wills that you can, because all details can help build a picture of the person's life and relationships.

Birth certificates give the name and occupations of the father, birthplace. Scottish records, available from Scotland's People, give additional information about the mother. The names of witnesses, parents and officiants on marriage certificates can all be helpful. Death certificates give a place and date of death, age of the person, cause of death, and who was with them when they died. Wills can give a good impression of the person's wealth, or otherwise, and an insight into their family relationships.

George Giles Vincent's will, for this book, was a mine of information. I discovered from it that he had investments in a tin mine in Cornwall, which helped explain where some of his wealth came from, and that he had been heavily subsidising two of his sons, who had health problems and consequent debts.

Family Search; www.familysearch.org (free of charge)

Free BMD; https://www.freebmd.org.uk/ (free of charge)

Find my Past; www.findmypast.co.uk; (with subscription)

Ancestry; www.ancestry.co.uk; (with subscription)

Scottish records; https://www.scotlandspeople.gov.uk/ (purchase credits and pay per item)

Birth, marriage and death certificates can be ordered from; https://www.gro.gov.uk/gro/content/certificates/ (fee per item)

Wills are available from https://probatesearch.service.gov.uk/#wills (fee per item)

Wills proved prior to 1858 might be at the National Archives; https://www.nationalarchives.gov.uk/ (fee per item)

Free online resources

There is an amazing amount of information online, much of it free. Historical works, maps, genealogical lists, school registers, and historic directories are just some of the treasures that might be relevant to your research.

British Library; https://www.bl.uk/

Google books; books.google.com

Hathi Trust; www.hathitrust.org/

Internet Archive; www.archive.org

Leicester University; https://le.ac.uk/library/special-collections/explore/historical-directories for historic area directories

Project Gutenberg; www.gutenberg.org/

Libraries and Archives

There are many kinds of archive; as well as the main county records offices, institutions, stately homes, schools and companies may keep their own records, and invariably the archivist is only too willing to help find the information you need.

Berkshire Records Office

Brighton College

Community of the Sisterhood of St Mary the Virgin, Wantage

Church of England Records Archive

Westminster Abbey Library

The public libraries of Wokingham, Reading and Brighton, all of whom gave additional access to online resources during lockdown.

Personal information

I am indebted to Simon Dear and Simon Pocock, who allowed me to see a copy of family information collated by their great-grandfather, Charles Greaves Vincent.

Also to the unknown person who left a handwritten note in a record of church services held at Helena House, who enabled me to find the story of Lucy May Owindia.

Software

I used an Access database to keep track of the 4,000 odd people in Emilia's life. Most of them don't get a mention in the finished work, but at the beginning, it's hard to tell who's important and who's not.

I also used My Family Tree software, which is freeware from Chronoplex Software, and available from the Microsoft Store.

And finally

Corroborate everything and always be prepared to change what you think you know. Primary sources can contain bias, different opinions and plain errors of fact. Allow for differences in the spellings of names, and that people didn't always give their correct age.

Even the same person may not write about the same thing the same way twice.

I found three versions of the story of Lucy May Owindia; the first was a handwritten piece of paper stuck in the back of a record book of church services held at Helena House. This book is in the keeping of the Berkshire Records Office. That version of the story turned out to have some inaccuracies; but the lady who was the original source of the story, Mrs Charlotte Selina Bompas, herself wrote two versions of the story, in an article in *"The Net"* in 1881 and in *"Owindia"* in 1890. In 1881, Lucy's father was named as Miktell. In 1890, he had become Michel. Was Mrs Bompas making his name easier for the reader in the later account? Or was it that a printer misread the name from her handwritten manuscript on one of the occasions? I used the name

"Michell" in this work, as the majority of the quotations are from *"Owindia"*, but that could be wrong. Some ambiguities cannot be resolved and just have to be lived with.

The tendency of some families to use the same names in successive generations can lead the researcher up the garden path; plus the fact that some names are simply very common.

Emilia had at least three relatives called "William Vincent;" her grandfather the Dean of Westminster, her uncle Rev. William St. Andrew Vincent, and her cousin, whom I called in my database "William junior junior." You'd think that "William St. Andrew Vincent" should be a distinctive enough name; but there is another individual of that name, and living in the same part of Sussex at the same time as Emilia's uncle. Since one was a watchmaker and one a clergyman, the two can be distinguished without too much head-scratching, but not all instances are so clear.

I spent a lot of time trying to trace Emilia's niece, Dorothea Vincent, because she seemed to disappear after the death of her father, Rev. Thomas Vincent in 1908. Records searches kept coming up with another Dorothea Vincent; but I was able to establish that Dorothea Vincent, musician and band leader from Guildford, was not the right lady, with the help of press reports in the British Newspaper Archive, where I found details of her parents and place of birth. At Find My Past, I found an overseas marriage of a Dorothea Vincent to a Rev. Herbert C. Muriel between 1916 and 1920, so from there I was able to find some references to Mrs Dorothea Muriel, her return to England, some subsequent addresses and her date of death. So far, there was nothing that definitely identified Mrs Muriel as Miss Vincent, Emilia's niece. The final piece of jigsaw came from Mrs Muriel's will, which helped me to match up the relatives from her list of legacies with the relatives I knew about from the Vincents' family tree.

So try not to wince at the cost of obtaining wills or other documents; they might just contain the missing jigsaw piece you are looking for.

Sources

[1] Alexander Mackay 'The Devil's Acre' in *Household Words*, Volume I, Magazine No.13, 22 June 1850, pp.297-301

[2] W.J. Loftie *Westminster Abbey*. London, Seeley & Co. 1890, p.4

[3] John Timbs, *Romance of London*, Volume 1. 1865, p.441

[4] *The Morning Post*, 9 April 1834, p.1

[5] Metropolitan Sanitary Commission. Third report; Minutes of Evidence taken before the Commissioners appointed to inquire whether any and what special means may be requisite for the improvement of the health of the metropolis. London, William Clowes & Sons. 1848, p.44. Available at https://books.google.com/

[6] Charles Dickens, *Our Mutual Friend*, in Charles Dickens, The Complete Novels, Kindle ed. 1864, p. 11166, location 158126

[7] Charles Dickens, *Our Mutual Friend,* p.11166, location 158126

[8] *Robsons London Directory*, 23rd edition. Robson & Co, London. 1842, p.204

[9] Charles Dickens, *David Copperfield,* in Charles Dickens, The Complete Novels, Kindle ed. 1850, p.7105, location 100867.

[10] John Nichols, *History and Antiquities of Leicestershire*, Vol 1, part 2. 1815, p.934

[11] John Sergeaunt, *Annals of Westminster School*. London, Methuen. 1898, p.128

[12] Sergeaunt, *Annals*, p.211

[13] George Giles Vincent, *An explanation of morality and of good and evil; or the Laws and Rules of Human Actions generally.* London, T Cadell & RH Evans. 1823, p.vi-vii. Available at https://books.google.com/

[14] Vincent, *An explanation of morality and of good and evil*, p.vii-viii

[15] Trowles, Tony, 'Vincent, William' in *Oxford Dictionary of National Biography*. Oxford University Press, 2012, available at https://doi.org/10.1093/ref:odnb/28316

[16] *Gentlemen's Magazine, Volume 86,* Ed. Sylvanus Urban. Jan to June 1816, p.64

[17] Information from personal email from Proprietary House Museum, Perth Amboy, New Jersey.

[18] *The Rugby Register.* Rugby, T Combe & Co. 1838, p.110-113

[19] Serio-Comic Sketches, Canterbury, 1791, quoted in Peter Tann, 'James Tappenden, Town Clerk of Faversham, attorney, banker, industrialist and bankrupt, 1742-1841.' *Archaelogia Cantiana* Vol. 115. 1995, p.213.

[20] Tann, James Tappenden, p.220-221

[21] *Records of the 54th West Norfolk Regiment.* Roorkee, printed at the Thomason Civil Engineering College Press. 1881, p.36 & 43

[22] Kentish Weekly Post and Canterbury Journal, 25 December 1807.

[23] Joseph Jackson Howard (ed) *Miscellanea Genealogica et Heraldica*, Volume II new series. 1877, p.240

[24] L.S. Pressnell. *Country Banking in the Industrial Revolution.* Oxford, Clarendon Press. 1956, p.328

[25] W.J. Loftie *Westminster Abbey.* London, Seeley & Co. 1890, p.10

[26] Charles Greaves Vincent. A short sketch of the life of the Rev. William Vincent DD, Dean of Westminster and Dean of the Order of the Bath. Unpublished personal document, 1914. Supplied by Simon Pocock.

[27] Death certificate, Richard Ignatius Robertson.

[28] *The Times*, 22 February 1847, p.12

[29] Dalby Herald and Western Queensland Advertiser, 11 January 1866, p. 2

[30] WW1 records of Margaret Agnes Josepha Robertson, WO/398/189, Available from https://www.nationalarchives.gov.uk/

31 *The Field*, Vol III, 6 June 1908.

32 A.M.W. Stirling (Ed). The Diaries of Dummer; Reminiscences of an old sportsman, Stephen Terry of Dummer. 1934, p. 121

33 A.M.W. Stirling (Ed). *The Diaries of Dummer*, p. 161

34 A.M.W. Stirling (Ed). *The Diaries of Dummer*, p. 123

35 A.M.W. Stirling (Ed). *The Diaries of Dummer*, p. 208

36 Death certificate, Jemima Tappenden.

37 Death certificate, Jenkin Edward Tappenden.

38 A.M.W. Stirling (Ed). *The Diaries of Dummer*, p. 309

39 1841 census, available from https://www.ancestry.co.uk/ or https://www.findmypast.co.uk/

40 Joseph Lemuel Chester. *The Marriage, Baptismal and Burial Registers of the Collegiate Church or Abbey of St. Peter, Westminster*. London, Private Edition. 1876, p.xi. Available at www.archive.org

41 Last Will and Testament of George Giles Vincent.

42 *The Times*, 24 March 1841, p.3

43 *The Digital Panopticon* Henry Brown b. 1814, Life Archive ID obpt18330411-82-defend682 (https://www.digitalpanopticon.org/life?id=obpt18330411-82-defend682) Version 1.2.1, consulted 11 January 2022.

44 Vincent, An explanation of morality and of good and evil. p.14-15

45 George Giles Vincent, An explanation of Moral rights; in a Practical View of the Subject and as Opposed to the Erroneous Idea of Natural Rights. London, Thomas Cadell. 1830, p.6

46 Richard Owen. *The Life of Richard Owen; by his grandson*, Volume 1. New York, D Appleton and Company. 1894, p. 329. Available at https://archive.org/

47 George Giles Vincent. An explanation of Moral rights, p. 84

48 'Richard Robertson', *Legacies of British Slavery* database, at http://wwwdepts-live.ucl.ac.uk/lbs/person/view/27376 [accessed 16 August 2021].

[49] St Pancras Parish register, 3 October 1843, in *London, England, Marriages and Banns, 1754-1921,* available from https://www.ancestry.co.uk/

[50] Barker, G. F. Russell. *The Record of Old Westminsters.* London, England: Chiswick Press. 1928, p. 952. Available at https://www.ancestry.co.uk/

[51] *The St. James's Chronicle,* 20-22 August 1833, p.1

[52] *The Morning Herald,* 1 January 1840, p.1

[53] *The Morning Herald,* 1 January 1840, p.1

[54] *The Times,* 18 March, 1839, p.5.

[55] *Norwich Mercury,* 23 March 1839, p.2

[56] *The Rugby Register.* Rugby, T Combe & Co. 1838, p.110 & 113

[57] Frederic H. Forshall, *Westminster School Past and Present.* London, Whyman & Sons. 1884, p.337. Available at https://archive.org/

[58] Forshall, p.64

[59] John Sergeaunt, *Annals of Westminster School.* London, Methuen & Co, 1898, p.233. Available at https://archive.org/

[60] Sergeaunt, p.233

[61] Henry L. Thompson, *Henry George Liddell, D.D., Dean of Christ Church, Oxford; a Memoir.* London, John Murray. 1899, p.88. Available at https://archive.org/

[62] Elizabeth Oke Gordon, *The Life and Correspondence of William Buckland, D.D.., FRS.* London, John Murray. 1899, p.230. Available at https://archive.org/

[63] Forshall, p.113

[64] *The Globe,* 26 June 1838, p.2

[65] *The Standard,* 26 June 1838, p.4

[66] Westminster Abbey Muniments, 51309A-11A, quoted in Fraser, Flora. *The Unruly Queen.* New York, First Anchor Books Edition. 1996, p.3

[67] Music at the Last Coronation, in *The Musical Times and Singing Class Circular,* Vol 43, no. 707, 1 January 1902, p.20. Available at http://www.jstor.org/stable/3369403

[68] Music at the Last Coronation, p.18

[69] *West Kent Guardian*, 26 May 1838, p.3

[70] *The Musical World,* Vol VIII, New Series, Vol 1. 21 June 1838, p.126-127. Available at https://archive.org/

[71] The Musical World, p.126-127

[72] *Morning Advertiser*, 27 June 1838, p.3

[73] *Morning Advertiser,* 27 June 1838, p.3

[74] Forshall, p. 451

[75] *The Globe,* 26 June 1838, p.2

[76] Bell's Life in London and Sporting Chronicle, 1 July 1838, p.3

[77] Bell's Life in London and Sporting Chronicle, 1 July 1838, p.3

[78] George Webbe Dasent, *Half a Life* Vol. 1. London, Chapman and Hall. 1874, p. 177. Available at https://archive.org/

[79] 1894. Rowland E. Prothero, *The Life and Correspondence of Arthur Penrhyn Stanley, Late Dean of Westminster.* New York, Charles Scribner's Sons. p.199-200. Available at https://archive.org/

[80] *The Globe,* 26 June 1838, p.2

[81] *Morning Post,* 3 July 1838, p. 5

[82] London Evening Standard, 26 June 1838, p.8

[83] The Morning Advertiser, 2 July 1838, p.4

[84] The Kilkenny Journal, 4 July 1838, p.1

[85] London Evening Standard, 26 June 1838, p.8

[86] *Morning Advertiser*, 2 July 1838, p.4

[87] London Courier and Evening Gazette, 10 July 1838, p.3

[88] M.C. & E.T. Bradley, *The Deanery Guide to Westminster Abbey,* 1895, p.12. Available at https://archive.org/

[89] Forshall, p.55

[90] Arthur Milman, *Henry Hart Milman, D.D.; Dean of St. Paul's, A Biographical Sketch.* London, John Murray. 1900, p. 165. Available at https://archive.org/

[91] Milman, p. 150

[92] London Metropolitan Archives; London, England; *London Church of England Parish Registers;* Ref. no. DW/T.0525. Available at https://www.ancestry.co.uk/

[93] Elizabeth Oke Gordon. The Life and Correspondence of William Buckland, p.7-8, 113-116. Available at https://archive.org/

[94] Gordon, p.171.

[95] Gordon, p.167.

[96] Gordon, p.217.

[97] John Ruskin, *Praeterita,* Vol. I. London, George Allen. 1907, p.313. Available at https://archive.org/

[98] George C. Bompas, *Life of Frank Buckland.* London, Smith, Elder & Co. 1885, p.8. Available at https://archive.org/

[99] George C. Bompas, p.69.

[100] Gordon, p.172.

[101] Metropolitan Sanitary Commission, p.61.

[102] Metropolitan Sanitary Commission, p.44

[103] Metropolitan Sanitary Commission, p.60

[104] Metropolitan Sanitary Commission, p.10

[105] Metropolitan Sanitary Commission, p.13

[106] Metropolitan Sanitary Commission, p.11

[107] Gordon, p.247

[108] Metropolitan Sanitary Commission, p. 44

[109] Death certificate of Mary Rohan.

[110] Thompson, p. 100

[111] Metropolitan Sanitary Commission, p. 58

[112] *The Weekly Chronicle*, 13 May 1848, p.4

[113] Death certificate of Georgiana Ewart.

[114] Metropolitan Sanitary Commission, p. 35

[115] Inscription in the North Cloister, Westminster Abbey

[116] Metropolitan Sanitary Commission, p. 36

[117] Metropolitan Sanitary Commission, p. 24

[118] Metropolitan Sanitary Commission, p. 45

[119] John Macrobin, M.D., An Introduction to the Study of Practical Medicine; being an outline of the leading facts and

principles of the science, as taught in a course of lectures delivered in the Marischal College of Aberdeen. First American edition, Philadelphia, A Waldie. 1841, p. 89. Available at https://archive.org/

[120] Macrobin, p. 97.

[121] Forshall, p. 85

[122] Gordon, p. 223

[123] George C. Bompas, p. 24

[124] George C. Bompas, p.27

[125] George C. Bompas, p. 66

[126] George C. Bompas, p. 74

[127] E.W. Watson, D.D., *Life of John Wordsworth*. London and New York, Longmans, Green & Co. 1915, p. 5. Available at https://archive.org/

[128] Thompson, p.100

[129] Gordon, p. 248

[130] The Weekly Chronicle, 13 May 1848, p.4

[131] Bell's Weekly Messenger, 14 May 1848, p.3

[132] George Hume Weatherhead, *An Account of the Beulah Saline Spa at Norwood, Surrey*. London, J. Hatchard & Son, W. Joy & S. Highley. 1832, p. 6

[133] Weatherhead, p. 9

[134] Edward J. Seymour, *The Nature and Treatment of Dropsy. Parts I & II, Anasarca & Ascites*. London, Longman, Rees, Orme, Brown, Green & Longman. 1837, pp. 89, 90, 91, 92, 99

[135] Death certificate of Emilia Elizabeth Vincent.

[136] Edna Healey, *Lady Unknown; The life of Angela Burdett-Coutts*. London, Sidgwick & Jackson, 1978, p. 98-99

[137] Rebecca Stott, *Theatres of Glass*. Short Books. 2003.

[138] Gordon, p. 253-254

[139] Last Will and Testament of George Giles Vincent.

[140] 1851 census

[141] Death certificate of George Vincent.

[142] Death certificate of Caroline Vincent.

[143] Death certificate of Francis William.

[144] Last Will and Testament of George Giles Vincent

[145] W.S.F. Pickering, *Anglo Catholicism; a study in religious ambiguity*. London and New York, Routledge. 1989, p. 43

[146] Russell, 1917, quoted in Pickering, p.109

[147] Anon, Butler of Wantage; his inheritance and his legacy. Westminster, Dacre Press. p.52

[148] 1871 Census

[149] *The Evening Standard*, 25 November 1862, p.5

[150] 1881 Census

[151] Cecilia Robinson, *The Ministry of Deaconesses*. London, Methuen & Co. 1898, p.137

[152] Robinson, p.146

[153] Robinson, p.139

[154] Anon, Butler of Wantage, p. 22

[155] Susan Mumm, *Stolen Daughters, Virgin Mothers; Anglican Sisterhoods in Victorian Britain*. London & New York, Leicester University Press. 1999, p. 82

[156] Mumm, p.64

[157] Sister Ann Frances Norton, *A history of the community of St. Mary the Virgin*. Durham Theses, Durham University. 1974, p.33. Available at http://etheses.dur.ac.uk/9849/.

[158] Sister Ann Frances Norton, *The Consolidation and expansion of the Community of St Mary the Virgin, Wantage, 1857 – 1907*. Thesis for the degree of M.Phil of the University of London, through King's College, London. 1978, p.85. Held in the archive of the Community of St. Mary the Virgin.

[159] Healey, p.116-117

[160] *London Evening Standard*, 24 August 1871, p.2

[161] *The Worcester Herald*, 26 August 1871, p.3

[162] Daniel J. R. Grey, 'What woman is safe…?: coerced medical examinations, suspected infanticide, and the response of the women's movement in Britain,1871–1881,' in *Women's History Review*, 2013, 22:3, 403-421, https://doi.org/10.1080/09612025.2012.726124

[163] Robert Eden, 'Help me, or I perish!': the plea for penitentiaries: a sermon preached by the Bishop of Moray and Ross; before the Church Penitentiary Association, at Saint James's Church, Piccadilly, on Thursday April 24, 1856. London: printed for the Association by Spottiswood & Co., New Street Square. 1856, p. 7

[164] Norton, A history of the community of St. Mary the Virgin, p. 20

[165] Sir Arthur Quiller-Couch, *Memoir of Arthur John Butler*. London, John Murray. 1917, p. 16

[166] Butler, Arthur J. Life and Letters of William John Butler; Late Dean of Lincoln, and sometime Vicar of Wantage. London, MacMillan and Co. 1898, p.48

[167] Rev. Thomas Vincent, An Account of the Year 1852 of St. Mary's Home for Penitents, at Wantage, Berkshire and an appeal for assistance towards its support and enlargement, by the chaplain. Oxford, John Henry Parker. 1853, p.17. Available at www.bl.uk

[168] Norton, A History of the Community of St. Mary the Virgin, p.42

[169] Rev. Thomas Vincent. *St Mary's Home for Penitents, Wantage, Berkshire; its first nine years*. Oxford and London, John Henry and James Parker. 1859, p.4-5. Available at www.bl.uk

[170] Vincent, St. Mary's Home for Penitents, p.19

[171] Norton, The Consolidation and expansion of the Community of St Mary the Virgin. 1978, p.33. Photo printed by kind permission.

[172] Norton, *A history*, p.64

[173] Vincent, *An account*, p.30

[174] Rev. William John Butler, personal journal entry for xvii Sunday after Trinity, 4 October, quoted in Norton, *The Consolidation and expansion of the Community of St Mary the Virgin*. 1978, p.34

[175] Norton, A History of the Community of St. Mary the Virgin, p. 42

[176] Christabel Coleridge, *Charlotte Mary Yonge; Her life and letters.* London, MacMillan & Co. 1903, p. 314

[177] Mumm, p. 205

[178] Mumm, p. 14

[179] *Reading Mercury,* 3 August 1872, p.6

[180] *Berkshire Chronicle,* 3 August 1872, p.5

[181] *Reading Mercury,* 22 March 1873, p.6

[182] *Reading Mercury,* 22 March 1873, p.6

[183] Arthur F. Leach, *A History of Bradfield College.* London, Henry Frowde, Oxford University Press, 1900, p.163

[184] *The Morning Post,* 21 September 1885, p.1

[185] *Reading Mercury,* 25 November 1876, p.2

[186] *Berkshire Chronicle,* 14 April 1883, p.8

[187] Death certificate of Mrs Ann Margaret Terry

[188] Florence Nightingale, *Notes on Nursing; what it is and what it is not.* London, Harrison and Sons. 1860, p. 37

[189] Nightingale, p.27

[190] 1841 census

[191] 1841 and 1851 Scottish Censuses, available from https://www.scotlandspeople.gov.uk/

[192] 1881, 1891 and 1901 censuses.

[193] 1871 census

[194] Death certificate, Louise Henriette Diday

[195] Last Will and Testament of Louise Henriette Diday

[196] 1881 census

[197] *Berkshire Chronicle,* 19 February 1881, p.6

[198] Ashley H. Robins & Sean L. Sellars, "Oscar Wilde's terminal illness: reappraisal after a century," in *The Lancet,* Vol. 356. 25 November 2000, p.1841-43. Available at https://doi.org/10.1016/S0140-6736(00)03245-1

[199] *Reading Observer,* 27 November 1880, p.4

[200] *The Guardian,* 15 January 1890, p.40

[201] Handwritten note attached to *Register of services (Helena House) 1959-1978* in 'All Saints Parish Records', held at Berkshire Records Office.

[202] Plans held at Lambeth Palace Library

[203] *Berkshire Chronicle,* 16 December 1882, p.5

[204] *The Hospital,* 12 February 1887, p.339

[205] Death certificate of Eliza Williams

[206] The Nursing Home report, quoted in *Berkshire Chronicle,* 24 September 1887, p.2

[207] Handwritten note attached to Register of services (Helena House)

[208] 1851 census

[209] Death certificate of Margaret Andrews

[210] Handwritten note attached to Register of services (Helena House)

[211] 1861 & 1871 census

[212] 1881 census

[213] The Reading Observer, 14 April 1883

[214] Death certificate of Fanny Belcher

[215] New Zealand birth records, available at https://www.ancestry.co.uk/

[216] *Reading Mercury,* 6 February 1869, p. 5

[217] *Berkshire Chronicle,* 27 February 1869, p. 6

[218] *Berkshire Chronicle,* 20 November 1869, p. 5.

[219] Death certificate of Eliza Slocombe

[220] *Berkshire Chronicle,* 13 December 1890, p.5

[221] Death certificate of Eliza Harriette Slocombe

[222] 1901 census

[223] Last Will and Testament of Eliza Harriette Slocombe

[224] Death certificate of Sarah Frith Swallow

[225] The Shrewsbury Chronicle, 3 May 1872, p.7

[226] 1901 census

[227] Brighton College Register, (1847-1922). Nos. 1-5000, with Brief Biographical Notes. Farncombe. 1922, p.116

[228] *Calendar of Prisoners for HM Prison, Preston.* 1880. Available at https://www.ancestry.co.uk/

[229] *The Islington Gazette,* 13 February 1883, p.2

[230] *The Taunton Courier,* 3 November 1886, p.7

[231] *New South Wales, Australia, Public Service Lists,* available at https://www.ancestry.co.uk/

[232] *The Bucks Herald,* 16 January 1892, p.3

[233] *The Guardian,* 1 March 1899, p.27

[234] 1945 register of electors, available at https://www.ancestry.co.uk/

[235] Death certificate of Edith Marion Satchell

[236] Handwritten note attached to Register of services (Helena House)

[237] Death certificate of Edith Marion Satchell

[238] 1891 census

[239] 1891 census

[240] 1901 census

[241] 1901 census

[242] 1891 and 1901 censuses

[243] Last Will and Testament of Emilia Vincent

[244] Charlotte Selina Bompas, *Owindia: A true tale of the Mackenzie River Indians.* London, Wells Gardner, Darton & Co. 1886, frontispiece. Available at https://archive.org/

[245] Last will and testament of Emilia Vincent

[246] Charlotte Selina Bompas, *Owindia,* p. 16-17.

[247] Charlotte Selina Bompas, Owindia, p. 38-43

[248] Charlotte Selina Bompas, "Diocese of Athabasca," in *The Net,* 1 September 1881, p. 134. Available at https://books.google.com/

[249] Charlotte Selina Bompas, Owindia, p. 58

[250] Charlotte Selina Bompas, "Mackenzie River Diocese, North-West America" in *The Net,* 1 June 1887, p.89. London, Bemrose & Sons. Available at https://books.google.com/

[251] *Reading Mercury,* 19 March 1887, p. 5

[252] Death certificate of Caroline Bonnett

[253] Death certificate of Lucy Mary (sic) Owindia

[254] Reading Borough Council cemetery records

[255] *Reading Mercury,* 31 March 1888, p. 2

[256] *Reading Mercury,* 28 July 1888, p. 2

[257] *Reading Mercury,* 8 December 1888, p. 2

[258] *Reading Mercury,* 8 December 1888, p. 2

[259] *Berkshire Chronicle,* 19 January 1889, p. 5

[260] *The Evening News,* 6 February 1890, p. 3

[261] *Reading Mercury,* 8 February 1890, p. 4

[262] *The Evening News,* 1 March 1890, p. 2

[263] *The Evening News,* 30 August 1890, p. 2

[264] T. Wakley & T. Wakley. *The Lancet, Volume II,* 30 November 1889. Available at https://books.google.com/

[265] *St. James's Gazette,* 26 November 1889, p.12

[266] *The Lancet,* 28 June 1890, p.1457.

[267] Lindenbach, B. D.; et al. (2007). "Flaviviridae: The Viruses and Their Replication". In Knipe, D. M.; P. M. Howley (eds.). *Fields Virology* (5th ed.). Philadelphia, PA: Lippincott Williams & Wilkins. p.1101

[268] *The Daily News,* 26 December 1889, p.5.

[269] *The Lancet,* 11 January 1890, p.105.

[270] *The Lancet,* 29 March 1890, p.731.

[271] *Lancashire Evening Post,* 26 December 1889, p.3

[272] *The Daily News,* 26 December 1889, p.5

[273] *The Reading Observer,* 4 January 1890, p.5.

[274] *Reading Mercury,* 6 February 1892, p.6

[275] Office of National Statistics at https://tinyurl.com/yw5e3mhw accessed 25 August 2021

[276] *The Morning Post,* 28 December, 1889, p.5

[277] *The Lancet,* 4 January 1890, p.57

[278] *The Lancet,* 11 January 1890, p.73

[279] The Faringdon Advertiser, 9 March 1895, p.3

[280] *The Sleaford Gazette,* 15 February 1890, p.7

[281] South Wales Daily News, 7 April 1890, p.5

[282] *Newbury Weekly News,* 30 November 1899, p.6

[283] *The Lancet*, 11 January 1890, p.73.

[284] *The Lancet*, 18 January 1890, p.167

[285] *The Morning Post*, 28 December, 1889, p.5

[286] *The Lancet*, 4 January 1890, p.55

[287] Berks and Oxon Advertiser, 3 January 1890, p.2

[288] *The Farringdon Advertiser,* 11 January 1890, p.2

[289] *The Reading Observer*, 4 January 1890, p.5

[290] *Berkshire Chronicle,* 18 January 1890, p.5

[291] *Reading Observer*, 11 January 1890, p.5

[292] *Reading Mercury*, 1 February 1890, p.4

[293] *The Lancet*, 10 May 1891, p.1018

[294] *The Lancet*, 10 May 1891, p.1018

[295] *The Lancet*, 10 May 1891, p.1018

[296] *The Lancet,* 7 June 1890, p.1236

[297] *Reading Mercury*, 23 January 1892, p.5

[298] *Reading Mercury*, 30 January 1892, p.4

[299] *Reading Mercury*, 6 February 1892, p.5

[300] *Reading Mercury*, 30 January 1892, p.4

[301] *Reading Mercury*, 16 April 1892, p.5

[302] *Reading Mercury*, 23 January 1892, p.5

[303] *Reading Mercury*, 15 February 1892, p.5

[304] 'Health of Reading' report, quoted in *Reading Mercury*, 12 March 1892, p.8

[305] *Reading Mercury,* 4 June 1892, p.8

[306] *Reading Mercury*, 10 December 1892, p.5

[307] *Reading Mercury*, 10 December 1892, p.5

[308] Leen Vijgen, Els Keyaerts, Elien Moe̎s, Inge Thoelen, Elke Wollants, Philippe Lemey, Anne-Mieke Vandamme, and Marc Van Ranst, 2005. Complete Genomic Sequence of Human Coronavirus OC43: Molecular Clock Analysis Suggests a Relatively Recent Zoonotic Coronavirus Transmission Event. In *Journal of Virology*, Vol. 79, No. 3, Feb. 2005, p. 1595–1604. Available at: https://journals.asm.org/journal/jvi

[309] Death certificate, Sarah Bryan

310 1891 census

311 *Berkshire Chronicle,* 25 November 1893, p.8 and *Reading Mercury,* 25 November 1893, p.4.

312 Helena Nursing Home accounts, reported in the *Reading Mercury,* 16 December 1893, p.4

313 The Helena Nursing Home Report, List of Subscribers and Balance Sheet for the Year 1930. Copy held in Reading Library, Reading, Berkshire.

314 Statutes for the Regulation and Management of the Helena Nursing Home, 1893, p.10. Copy held in Reading Public Library.

315 Statutes for the Regulation and Management of the Helena Nursing Home, 1928, p. 6. Copy held in Reading Public Library

316 *The Homeward Mail,* 11 May 1868, p.414

317 *The Builder,* 26 January 1878, p.89

318 Find a Grave, database and images [https://www.findagrave.com/memorial/177721460/mary-prescott accessed 20 October 2021], memorial page for Mary Prescott (unknown–18 Dec 1896), *Find a Grave Memorial ID 177721460,* citing St. Thomas Cathedral, Mumbai (Bombay), Maharashtra, India ; Maintained by BobBoston (contributor 46926159) .

319 Death certificate of Rev. Thomas Vincent

320 1911 census

321 Death certificate of Emilia Vincent

322 Last Will and Testament of Emilia Vincent

323 The Helena Nursing Home Report, List of Subscribers and Balance Sheet for the Year 1930. Copy held in Reading Library.

324 *The Reading Standard,* 29 October 1954, p.3

325 *Reading Evening Post,* 15 June 1982, p.8

Printed in Great Britain
by Amazon